PROBLEM
PEOPLE
AT WORK

THE ESSENTIAL SURVIVAL GUIDE FOR

DEALING WITH BOSSES, COWORKERS,

EMPLOYEES, AND OUTSIDE CLIENTS

PROBLEM PEOPLE AT WORK

MARILYN WHEELER

PRESIDENT OF MARILYN WHEELER
AND ASSOCIATES

ST. MARTIN'S GRIFFIN
NEW YORK

Design by Junie Lee

Library of Congress Cataloging-in-Publication Data

Wheeler, Marilyn.
    Problem people at work : the essential survival
  guide to dealing with bosses, coworkers, employees,
  and outside clients / Marilyn Wheeler.
      p. cm.
    ISBN 0-312-13148-8 (pbk.)
    1. Managing your boss. 2. Problem employees.
  3. Interpersonal communication. 4. Interpersonal
  relations. I. Title.
  HF5548.83.W48 1995
  650.1'3—dc20   95-2108
                                                CIP

First St. Martin's Griffin Edition: May 1995

10 9 8 7 6 5 4 3 2 1

CONTENTS

CHAPTER 6   55
PASSIVE-AGGRESSIVE BEHAVIOR PROBLEMS

CHAPTER 7   72
PROCRASTINATING BEHAVIOR PROBLEMS

CHAPTER 8   92
NEGATIVE-COMPLAINING BEHAVIOR
PROBLEMS

ACKNOWLEDGMENTS

I am grateful to all the "teachers" I have had who have challenged, informed, supported, and taught me.

For the development of this book, I am grateful to all the seminar participants who have shared their most personal and difficult experiences. To the California Mart, which gave me the opportunity to learn, through my ten-year employment, how to manage and deal constructively with many problem people at work. To the people at the International Institute of Research, who had the confidence to give me the label of the "difficult employee doctor" while sending me around the world to help others. To my daughters, Michelle Brusseau and Tracy Wheeler, who have always been there to support me regardless of how the future appeared. To my dear friends, Marilyn Beker, Joan Cernich, and Sue Freeman, whose encouragement has kept my path light. And to Robert Weil, senior editor at St. Martin's Press, who said yes to my book.

INTRODUCTION

It was day one of a new job. No . . . more than day one of a new job, day one of a major career plateau. Today was the beginning of what I had worked so very hard for: the final goal, the title, recognition, and respect I deserved. What could go wrong? I felt terrific—proud and excited to be at such an important point. Anxious to meet all the people who would certainly support me and encourage me to success.

Arriving at the impressive thirteen-story building, I was directed to the management parking lot, thinking all the time, "Yes, I have arrived." All around me were professional people, perfectly dressed, scurrying around, going up and down escalators to their respective offices. *They'll know who I am one day,* I thought. I did not sense even a hint of the trouble that lay ahead.

My first meeting was with the senior vice president of the corporation, Mr. Ted Cooper. Mr. Cooper was my boss's boss, not my direct boss. He had not been part of the interview process, so this would be our first encounter. I knew he was very important. *How nice of him,* I thought, *to greet me on this very important day.*

I entered his office. A huge rectangular desk stood between us, with a large oriental carpet under the desk and chairs. I wasn't quite sure whether to wait at the edge of the carpet or sit down, as he was on the telephone and I did not want to interrupt. I felt awkward standing, so I took a seat. He continued talking in a rather aggressive tone, not giving me any eye contact, but I knew that would all change as soon as he hung up the phone. I began looking at the collection of pictures on the wall: a President or two; some photos of marathon races he had run in; family pictures. He was still on the phone. I did not want to squirm but I was beginning to feel confused about what I was doing here. Kathy, his secretary, ran in and put something on his desk. On her way she gave me the "I am sure he will be with you in a minute" look, and I relaxed a bit.

Finally Mr. Cooper put down the receiver. He leaned back in his chair and looked at me, and the questions began. "You know, Marilyn, your predecessor was terrific. How do you think you can be as good as her?" *What!* I thought. *How do I know? I haven't even started!* He continued without much concern for my answers. "We all wish she had not left, but she was offered a wonderful opportunity that she couldn't turn down." By this time my heart was beginning to sink a bit. The conversation continued with me explaining my expectations, goals, capabilities. Finally, Mr. Cooper was done with me, but he had one parting comment I will never forget: "Marilyn, you'll never make it here." I responded by telling him that he was wrong, and then departed.

The person who had arrived in the morning all fired up with anticipation was gone. Now she was afraid—*What if I can't make it?*—and depressed—*I wonder if I've made a mistake. I want to be here for a very long time . . . now what?*

There is a happy ending to this story, and I have Ted Cooper to thank for it. After tears, anxiety, and sleepless nights, I decided to prove to him and myself that he was wrong. I *could* do the job and would show that I could do it better than my "terrific" predecessor. It seemed that my biggest obstacle was going to be dealing with problem people. I knew that if I did not learn how to communicate with this man and others like him, I would be chewed up and spit out, and my career would be over. I would be a miserable person if I could not learn to cope with bosses, customers, and associates who were not there to support me as I had previously imagined. The industry I had chosen was filled with aggressive, hungry people, many of them with the philosophy of "I win and you lose."

The first step, I decided, was to sign up for two courses in assertiveness training. This was pretty new to me, and I hoped it would give me the tools I needed. I kept my goal very clear: I wanted this job, this career to work. I knew *I had to change*. I could not hope that all the difficult people in my life would change—there were far too many of them!

I began to use my assertiveness skills as soon as I learned them. I had been in my new job approximately six months, and felt that Ted was available to listen if I could figure out how to get and keep his attention. I was aware that he had attended some communication seminars, so I decided to take the chance and approach him. (This may not, however, be an appropriate approach for others in a different working environment.)

The day after one of the classes, I went into his office and walked up to the desk (I did not stand at the edge of the carpet). I told Ted that I was taking assertiveness training in order to learn how to communicate more effectively with him. He seemed interested in what I was saying, and I breathed a little easier. He asked what I had learned. I explained how his carpet and huge desk were power signals that intimidated people who came into his office: they never knew whether to approach, stand, or sit. I went on to point out that during meetings he was always answering the phone, and that this made me feel that what I had to say was not important. At that moment the phone rang and he started to pick it up, then he stopped and gave a little laugh. I also told him that I realized that he needed brief answers without a lot of explanation, and so if he wanted any more information about what I had learned, he was to ask me. Then I left.

There were many challenges and changes over the next ten years while I worked for this corporation (Ted redecorated his office with a round table and no carpet). Because of my experience here, after much research and training, I decided to start my own business helping others deal with difficult people and situations.

I hope that this book will help you in your personal and professional life. Remember that it is an ongoing process. You must work at it every day. When you slip and feel as if you have been trapped or hooked by a difficult person, don't give up: instead you should learn from the experience, and remember that as you change, everything around you will change too.

PROBLEM
PEOPLE
AT WORK

CHAPTER ONE

BAD DAY, BAD WEEK, BAD BEHAVIOR

You feel good when you can spend time with people who are pleasant, easy to get along with, honest, reliable and willing to listen to a different point of view. Then there are those people who are argumentative, moody, aggressive, and just plain obnoxious. Whether they are a colleague, boss or family member, they can make life miserable! The following statements are from some of the thousands of people who have attended my seminars on dealing with these types of people:*

SITUATION 1. The personnel director is a lying, blackmailing, slippery person who will be nice to your face and talk about you behind your back. My immediate boss is weak and abdicates her

---

*At the author's Problem People and How to Deal with Them seminars, each participant writes a short description of his or her most difficult situation.

responsibilities for dealing with the general office to me. I feel so frustrated, I think the best thing is just to leave. *Karen.*

SITUATION 2. I work for thirteen partners, all with a different way of doing things. All want to manage the firm and I have to try to keep all of them happy. Help! *Kate.*

SITUATION 3. When trying to describe my most difficult situation, it seems similar to thinking about what is my favorite film, record, etc.—it changes by mood. I'll bend the question to what is my most frustrating situation. I imagine my problem is common amongst large organizations—how to deal with problems that are cross-organizational when my goals/objectives are not those of other areas. How do I get what I want? Persuasion, bullying, blackmail, or threats? *Sam.*

The desperation and frustration felt by these people is obvious.

What can *you* do to improve or change your situation? How can you feel better about what you're doing, keep your self-esteem, and communicate with these people who seem to be the problem? You have already taken the first step by picking up this book. The acknowledgment that there is a problem and the desire to improve it will begin the process of change. When a person is really difficult, all your wishing that he/she will change, or all your wonderful friendly behavior will probably not make a bit of difference. Generally, keep your distance and watch the game being played. Learn to play that game to the best of your ability, so communication will be as good as possible. The following chapters will help you understand these communication games and make you feel more confident in dealing with your difficult person.

Before we go any further, it is very important to understand the difference between problem behavior and healthy conflict. If you are concerned with keeping everything calm and not causing any waves, you may view all conflict as problem behavior.

There is a difference. Conflict is a healthy action when it is not an attack or perceived as such. Study the following table to help you make the distinction between problem behavior and healthy conflict. Let's go back to the *Situations 1, 2,* and *3* and diagnose whether these are healthy conflict or problem behavior.

SITUATION 1. The personnel director does not tell the truth and the boss is weak. Karen is considering leaving.

This situation is very stressful, to say the least, and both the personnel director and the boss are exhibiting poor behavior. The

PROBLEM BEHAVIOR	HEALTHY CONFLICT
Takes the energy and focus away from the important issues	Opens ideas for discussion even if they are controversial
Decreases productivity	Increases productivity and results
Lowers group attitude and hurts self-esteem	Supports self-esteem
Stops healthy discussions	Leads to solving the problems
Creates an atmosphere of "I win and you lose"	Creates an atmosphere of "I win and you win"
Causes fear and distrust between people	Ultimately lowers stress and anxiety

personnel director has stopped healthy discussion, creating an atmosphere of "I win and you lose" and causing fear and distrust among people. The boss, having a different style of difficult behavior, is decreasing productivity, taking energy and focus away from the important issues and not taking responsibility. Karen seems to be the victim caught between two difficult people.

Leaving does not seem to be the best solution in this time of economic decline and scarcity of jobs. Karen must do everything in her power to improve the situation so that she can stay and enjoy her work.

First, when communicating with the personnel director, Karen should ask questions whenever she feels or knows that he is being dishonest. If she stands there and does nothing, this simply will reinforce his behavior. She should ask questions starting with *why, when, who, what, where,* and *how much.* Of course he will resent it, but she must keep asking in order to clarify his replies and break his habit. She should ask with the attitude of "I am so interested/concerned about what you're telling me. I just need more information . . ."

Here is a sample conversation:

> *Personnel Director:* "The forms were put on Sally's desk just as you requested."
>
> *Karen (who knows this is not true):* "That is puzzling. Sally has no knowledge of them. When did you give them to her?"
>
> *Personnel Director:* "I am sure it was last Friday."
>
> *Karen:* "Who received them?"
>
> *Personnel Director:* "I don't remember. Why are you bothering me?"
>
> *Karen:* "I am very concerned about the confusion, as these are very important. Can you help clear this up for me?"
>
> *Personnel Director:* "Oh, this is ridiculous . . . I'll find them and give them to you this afternoon."

Karen: "How much time will you need? Will one hour be enough for you to find them?"

Personnel Director: "I suppose so."

Karen: "Thanks, what time will I get them?"

Personnel Director: "I said in an hour, didn't I?"

Karen: "Thanks, that will be great."

Notice that Karen did not call him a "lying, blackmailing, slippery person," but they both know she is aware of what is going on and will not let it go by without attention. Karen must do this every time in order to break the habit.

When dealing with the boss, Karen must stop taking the responsibility that is not hers. She needs to be able to say "no" in an appropriate, assertive manner. Learning to respond by taking a minute or two to think her answer through instead of reacting instantly will move her closer to the appropriate "no." Saying "yes" is keeping her in the victim mode. Karen may be saying "yes" because she wants to be liked and appreciated, but it's not working. The boss will not like her new behavior. Karen will have to be prepared with good reasons and ready to weather the storm. She should have a "To Do" list every day, and when she is given a task that is not hers, she should point to the list and ask, "Which one of these would you like to delegate or eliminate to fit in the new project?" Eventually her boss will become stronger by taking her own responsibility. When this happens she is likely to bring about more direct communication with the personnel director, and in turn this will stop the behind-the-back talking and lying.

These solutions will take time and consistency. It takes at least twenty-one days to begin to change a habit—three whole weeks! Trying once or twice and then giving up will not accomplish anything. Sometimes it can feel like you have to go through a lot of rough water before you come to the calm lake, but it is always worth it.

> **Note:** It is very important to check on your own attitude. A negative attitude of "don't bother me" can cause conflict. Much of the time we receive what we reflect.

SITUATION 2. Dealing with thirteen different partners.

This situation appears to be healthy conflict. There are many discussions of new ideas and issues, productivity is increasing all the time, and self-esteem is high. The stress comes more from time limitations than from problem behavior.

Kate's biggest problem is dealing with thirteen different personalities. She feels like a chameleon, always changing color to fit the situation but never quite sure which color is correct. Kate can use more information to know exactly what color (or communication style) to use.

After dealing with thousands of people and researching communication techniques thoroughly, I have categorized communication styles into four types, which are described below. You can and probably do communicate in more than one style and the same is true for your difficult person. The goal is to be a little of all four. The more you can communicate in all four styles, the more balanced you are and the more people you will be able to deal with. Here are the four profiles:

1. The Bumper Sticker Communicator.

Visualize a bumper sticker. Bumper stickers say something in five words or less and are meant to have an immediate impact! The Bumper Sticker Communicator is the same. He gives and wants information in short sentences. If you go on and on, this person will become rude, withdraw his attention, and become hostile. He works quickly with only the goal in mind. He is not sensitive to personal feelings and is known to cause subordinates to cry. The Bumper Sticker Communicator is usually in a leadership position (the boss). The Bumper Sticker is very good at demonstrating power and being the boss is definitely a power position.

The Bumper Sticker Communicator is an achiever. He can, and usually does, make a lot of money. The down side is that he also can lose large amounts of money because he is a risk taker. His risk-taking personality has little patience for those who do not carry the same philosophy.

Ted Cooper, described in the introduction, is an example of a true Bumper Sticker Communicator.

The way to deal with this person is to be concise and to the point, speaking in a clear and confident voice. If you feel as if you are leaving out important information by giving a Bumper Sticker Communicator the short version, let him ask questions, or else outline the specifics on paper and leave it with him to read. A friend relayed to me a statement about this type of person, "They just want the baby, not the delivery!" Be prepared before approaching a Bumper Sticker Communicator with ideas or suggestions. This will give you the appearance of self-confidence even if you really feel nervous. Do not expect the Bumper Sticker Communicator to compliment or validate you or your ideas. This expectation can cause you to feel disappointed. Be confident in your own work and yourself. If you want validation or support, go to the Caretaking Communicator or the Cellular Phone Communicator.

Typical behavior displayed by a Bumper Sticker Communicator:

Self-sufficient

Authoritarian

Goal-directed

Dominant

Assertive to aggressive

Likes control

Fast worker

Impatient

Dislikes indecision

How to improve communication with a Bumper Sticker Communicator:

Be brief.

Be assertive.

Speak clearly.

Move fast.

Have self-confidence.

Have goals established.

2. The Caretaking Communicator

The Caretaking Communicator is very nice and wants to help everyone. She likes to tell very long stories and you could find yourself cornered. If you asked her about a movie, she may tell you everything about it from the first scene to the last credit, when all you really wanted to know is if it was a mystery or love story. The Caretaking Communicator will be the person who brings goodies into the office for everyone to share. She may arrange the special events when others just don't have the time. Her office or desk probably has pictures of family and friends in a variety of frames. *The decorator-placed family photos on the wall do not fall in this category!* The candy bowl sitting on the corner of the desk is an invitation for anyone to come and be nurtured.

The Caretaking Communicator does not like to carry the responsibility for the success or failure of projects. She is a great support person, but prefers not to be a leader. She will work as hard as you need her to work as long as she feels appreciated and supported.

You need to be sensitive to her needs. If she is rambling on about something that seems totally unimportant to you, and you think rude behavior will get the message across for her to stop, think again. Be very polite and concerned, but ask for the "short version" and mention that time is limited. If this does not work, watch when she takes a breath and then you jump in and gently direct the conversation where you need to go. A friend shared with me that when he and his wife (a Caretaking Communicator) are driving their car on the freeway, and she is explaining something, he tells her she has to finish the story by their exit!

Give clear directions for the work you need done and be willing to answer questions through the process of completion. This is the way she gets support and validation while working.

A question asked often in my seminars is, "What if the Caretaking Communicator is your boss and you can never get your work done because he or she is always coming into your office and won't leave?"

First, you must tell the person you are busy and will be able to talk later. If this does not deter him or her, then avoid eye contact and keep working. Just give slight sounds of acknowledgment but keep working. It will make you uncomfortable but the person usually gets the message. Another method is to stand up when he or she enters. This will give the appearance that you are leaving and only have a minute to hear the message. If this does not work, then you leave and go to the copy machine or go get a cup of coffee. Break the person's habit of knowing that you are the available person for him or her to talk with. Do set a specific time to spend with this individual on a regular basis. Remember the Caretaking Communicator gives nurturing because he or she wants it!

Typical behavior displayed by a Caretaking Communicator:

Accepting

Slow and steady

Tells personal feelings

Slow to take risk

Friendly

Helpful

Supportive

Nonconfrontive

Personal relationships important

How to improve communication with a Caretaking Communicator:

Be patient.

Be sensitive.

Plan time to listen.

Show personal feelings.

Ask for the short story (gently).

Give him or her recognition.

Do not embarrass him or her.

3. The Cellular Phone Communicator.

Can you guess? This person loves to talk to people. A picture of this person might portray him walking around with a cellular phone connected to his ear because he does not want to miss any opportunity to talk. Totally different from the Caretaker, he is more entertainer. He tends to be the center of attention, works on more than one project at a time, and is fast-moving and fun. He is often disorganized, and his office can seem to be chaotic. However, he knows exactly where everything is and you had better not move a thing! He gets bored if there is too much structure. He is a risk taker, similar to the Bumper Sticker, but the difference is his risk-taking tendency can come from dreams rather than research. Other words he might say are, "I have always wanted to do ——— (you fill in the blank) and so I will just do it because one never knows when life will end!" The amazing thing about the Cellular Phone Communicator is that most of the time these risks succeed! The reason is he has an endless source of energy and does not give up once the risk has been taken.

One of his downfalls is that many times he skips steps when working on a project because he wants the results the fastest way possible. For example, he will do steps 1, 2, 3, then skip 4 and 5, do 6, skip 7, and do 8, 9, and 10 . . . yea, he's done! He is done, but sometimes the skipped steps can backfire, causing inconveniences or time lost because he must redo his work.

When you communicate with the Cellular Phone Communicator, speak in a very positive way, faster than usual. Bring up ideas and goals but don't get stuck in all the research information, as this can bore him. He loves talking about himself, his work projects, his personal life, or just about anything. So ask him questions about himself, remembering it is one of his favorite subjects. Do not point out all the reasons why something will not work unless you want to aggravate him because he will look at you as a loser and a pessimist. Personal feelings are important to the Cellular Phone Communicator, therefore be willing to share yours.

Typical behavior displayed by a Cellular Phone Communicator:

Extrovert

Fast-moving

Talkative

Entertaining

Works on many projects at one time

Friendly

Optimistic

Exaggerates

Risk taker

How to improve communication with a Cellular Phone Communicator:

Talk faster than normal.

Be upbeat.

Share ideas and the big picture.

Don't get stuck in details.

Move quickly.

Be friendly.

Share personal stories that interest him or her.

Be willing to risk.

4. The Technocratic Communicator.

Unlike the Cellular Phone Communicator, the Technocratic Communicator tends to be quiet. The Technocrat must be sure that she carries out each step perfectly before she can go on to the next. She gets her information from research and data rather than from verbal communication. Organization could be her middle name. Everything must be in a specific place and order even at the cost of deadlines. Her desk, if she is an extreme Technocratic Communicator, would be clear of any papers or work material. In fact, you might ask if anyone works here!

She, like the Caretaking Communicator, is usually in a support position. The difference is she does not want or need attention. She just wants to do her job and be left alone. The Technocrat hates to divulge personal details about herself and thinks that other people talk too much. She prefers to spend time with people who can teach her something new or increase her knowledge. Sometimes her analytical mind can not see the easier way to accomplish a project which causes her to move slower than her co workers may like.

When talking to a Technocratic Communicator be very specific. Tell her exactly where you got the information, research, data, etc. Do not ask personal questions. Talk more slowly and allow her time to respond. Don't fill in the silences for the Technocrat, just sit back and be patient. Do not look over her shoulder to check on accuracy because it will just slow her down, and, besides, if she is a Technocratic Communicator, her work is correct. You will want to give specific deadlines and let her know how urgent these schedules actually are. Help her to understand that sometimes you are looking for "good enough," not perfect!

Typical behavior displayed by a Technocratic Communicator:

Precise

Organized

Quiet

Works alone

Slow to change

Problem solver

Cautious

Judgmental

Slow-moving

How to improve communication with a Technocratic Communicator:

Have facts and figures.

Don't share personal feelings.

Proceed one step at a time.

Have backup material.

Be organized.

Recognize his or her desire for perfection.

Don't discuss big-picture dreams.

Move slow.

Be patient.

Look at the box (on page 15) containing the four styles of communication. As I mentioned at the beginning of this chapter, you are likely to communicate in more than one style. The style that is diagonal to your most predominant style is usually your most difficult person to deal with. Example if you are strongly a Cellular Phone Communicator, your diagonal style is the Technocratic. This would be your most difficult behavior to understand. Also, you are normally a combination of one or two styles which are adjacent to your predominant one. For example, if you are a Bumper Sticker Communicator, you may also have some Technocratic and/or Cellular Phone Communicator as part of your personality.

Cellular Phone Communicator	Bumper Sticker Communicator
Caretaking Communicator	Technocratic Communicator

The following conversation may help you understand how differences can be misunderstood. The following conversation was between a Technocratic Communicator and a Cellular Phone Communicator following a breakup of a personal relationship.

T.C.: "I always thought you were so rude, always talking about your life. It felt like you never listened to me. However, now when I look back, I realize how you must have thought I was terribly boring because I never said anything. I always felt uncomfortable jumping in. I wanted to be invited!"

C.P.C.: "You're right. I never thought you had anything to say. When I would ask, how was your day, you would say it was fine. So, I would tell you everything about my day while you sat quiet. All the time I thought you had nothing to say, never realizing if I had just remained quiet when I asked you, and given you a little more time to respond, you would have opened up. I just wanted the conversation at my pace and wasn't patient."

Understanding communication styles is extremely helpful. If you are willing to look at your opposite communication style from the perspective of his or her strengths instead of what is not in alignment with your strengths, the relationship, personal or business, will definetly improve.

SITUATION 3. Sam's problems change according to his moods, but his biggest problem is that his goals and objectives are not the same as those of others.

I had a chuckle over this situation. Sam is very perceptive and honest. Our moods can certainly affect difficult situations. The situation that Sam describes could be either problem behavior or healthy conflict, depending on Sam's approach. Out of Sam's four choices—persuasion, bullying, blackmailing, or threats—persuasion would be the healthiest way to solve the problem. It may take longer, but the results would by far surpass those of the other methods. Bullying, blackmail, and threats can bring about temporary results, but the longer-term anger and frustration would cause a breakdown or elimination of teamwork and honest communication.

Having the philosophy of "I win and you win" instead of "I win and you lose" (or "we both lose") is the best way of changing people's minds. "I win and you win" does not mean "I am happy and you are happy"; it means that there is a give and take in which both parties are basically satisfied. They have each gained some ground while also having had to relinquish some points in other areas.

Whenever you are opposed to the goals of another part of the organization, ask yourself the following questions before you attempt to change the minds of the people involved. Your answers will help you decide how appropriate and healthy this communication will be.

1. Do I believe it is in the best interests of the organization to understand my point of view?

2. Is this a personal issue: Do I just need to be heard?

3. Will the outcome be worth the time and effort I intend to invest?

4. Would my time be better spent on supporting projects/goals in progress?

5. Are there more important changes that I want to discuss than this one?

6. Do I need always to be right?

Note: Seek first to understand and then to be understood.

CHAPTER TWO

COULD THE PROBLEM BE YOU?

There is a common thread running through each group that attends my seminars: many are there because they were sent by someone who saw them as difficult but did not have the courage to tell them. These people come to learn to deal with others, but discover that they themselves are the problem.

The most obvious example of this was David, who sat in the front row of a seminar and proudly announced that the way he got what he wanted was by intimidation and aggression. He claimed that his method always worked: the people he dealt with did not like confrontation, so he got what he wanted. He was proud of his behavior and did not see that it mattered how it was affecting others. (We will discuss this type of aggressive behavior in Chapter 4.)

This example is extreme, but many of us have a blind spot

about how we may be part of the problem. Answer the following questions to determine whether you are part of the problem or part of the solution.

1. Are you objective, willing to look at the issue from a point of view other than your own?

2. Do you listen without interrupting?

3. Do you speak in an ordering, directing, or commanding manner?

4. Do you interrogate (pounding, continuous, aggressive questioning) instead of questioning with interest?

5. Do you threaten?

6. Do you express your views assertively?

7. Do you bring up problems without offering solutions?

8. Do you take everything personally?

9. Is your speaking tone sincere and clear?

10. Is your voice loud enough for others to hear and respect your view but not too loud?

11. Do you fail to plan for the inevitable?

12. Do you react instead of respond?

13. Do you transfer personal problems to the workplace?

14. Do you judge others?

15. Are you willing to change?

If you answered "yes" to questions 1, 2, 6, 9, 10, and 15, and "no" to questions 3, 4, 5, 7, 8, 11, 12, 13, and 14, you are clearly part of the solution. It is likely that there are some areas in which you can see room for improvement. Don't get depressed. Instead, start by watching how you communicate, respond (not react), and think under pressure. Make small adjustments in order to make yourself a more positive and productive communicator.

When you find yourself in a difficult situation, ask yourself these questions in order to analyze where the problem is.

1. How often does this difficult situation arise? Rarely, often, or most of the time? If it happens rarely, it is probably just a bad day. If it occurs often or most of the time, the problem should be dealt with immediately. (There is specific information in the following chapters on how to deal with difficult situations.)

2. Do you have a personal prejudice about the person or situation? Be sure that you are evaluating the situation based on actual information, not on personal feelings.

3. How does this person view you? Does she think that you are the problem? Put yourself in her place before reacting. The golden rule of communication is: Do unto others as they would have you do unto them.

4. Can you be specific about what you want changed? The more specific and realistic you are, the more likely it is that you will be able to accomplish the change.

On the surface in the following situation, it looks as if the boss is difficult. Let's investigate further.

SITUATION 4. My boss asks a question that requires a lengthy answer. He does not listen, then complains, "You do not talk to me." *Mary.*

It's pretty obvious that Mary's boss falls into the category of Bumper Sticker Communicator. It is true that he could be insensitive, but let's take a look at Mary. Is she being objective? Is she taking things personally? What about the tone of her voice? Is it too soft or whining? Mary's response to her boss's questions is obviously a part of the problem. She feels that a lengthy answer is needed, even though her boss is not listening! This is the first clue and the most important one. Her boss is not listening because she is not communicating in a way that he can respond to. Mary feels that it is important for her to tell everything she knows and feels about the question, but in fact she needs to give short, concise answers. Mary can begin to be part of the solution by:

1. Shortening her answers.

2. Writing down any pertinent information (in outline form, not too lengthy) that she feels he must have.

3. Stating that he should ask for any further information he might need.

4. Leaving his office quickly, not lingering.

Why would the boss complain that Mary does not talk to him when it seems as if she may actually talk too much? When Mary feels she has not been heard in the first place, she closes down and withdraws, making a bad situation worse. Mary needs to work on not taking the boss's behavior personally. Remember that you cannot change someone else. You can only change yourself, and by doing so, the other person will also begin to change.

I understand that it is difficult to look at yourself as part of the problem when someone is making you feel bad. But you must try to examine your situation carefully. If you know someone who gets on beautifully with your problem person, ask them how they do it. If you're brave, also ask them how well they communicate with you.

• EXERCISE IN PERSPECTIVE

Do the following exercise in perception in order to help you understand yourself and your difficult person better.

Think of some people whose differences are hard for you to accept or understand. Pick one of those people and think for a moment about the things that irritate you. Now shift your point of view. Imagine that you are in this person's body and mind. You now have their eyes, brain, and feelings. You now see your true self from his or her perspective, from the center of who he or she is. What would irritate you about you if you were that person? Write down four things that you think another person would find hard to understand or accept about you.

You won't know how accurate you have been unless you are able to ask the person that you had in mind. However, you have done something significant. You have opened your mind to the possibility of seeing things from another perspective. If you practice this at least once with each person you find difficult to deal with, you will definitely be part of the solution.

CHAPTER THREE

ACHIEVE YOUR FREEDOM STATE

What is your Freedom State? It is a state of mind, a specific way of thinking, behaving, and communicating that can help you significantly in any difficult situation. If you read no further than this chapter, you will have gained valuable information to help you with your most stressful and challenging situations. As opposed to the external communication styles described previously, this chapter deals with internal thinking processes. When presenting this technique at seminars, there is immediate recognition from attendees that this is a method they can use to bring about an overall change in the way they communicate and react.

Before explaining exactly how you reach your Freedom State, I'll explain the two other communication states you use and how they can be positive or self-destructive in the workplace.

Immature State.
This does not mean you are immature if you react in this way; it simply means that you respond to difficult situations emotionally.

The positive side of communicating in the Immature State would be acting spontaneous, open or just having fun. In the work environment, you would be the person who makes people laugh or you may come up with great, or at least unique, ideas.

Example: Dave, who was attending a management seminar, was demonstrating the fun side of the Immature State. He would play off words with double meaning and make everyone laugh. He was very open and didn't mind being the butt of a joke. He would rock back in his chair and make comments to his neighbor while others were talking. During a break I discovered that Dave had had a close call with death. That experience had added to his already open personality a dimension of "don't take anything seriously." I must add, though, that Dave was very willing to quiet down if a serious request was made.

The destructive side of the Immature State is demonstrated by withdrawing either emotionally or physically. When reacting in the Immature State, you may find yourself feeling scared or victimized. You may avoid conflict at all costs because even the thought gives you an upset stomach. You may feel you have no control, tears may well up in your eyes, you might feel small. You may want to run away or, alternatively, you just don't know what to do, a total blank. You have trouble holding eye contact and may clasp or wring your hands. The tendency to get into the destructive Immature State happens when the difficult person is being aggressive, hostile, reprimanding, or controlling. Communication is off-balance at this point with the aggressive person pounding down the person who has responded in the Immature State.

Controlling State.

This is the opposite of the Immature State. Your responses are automatic (not emotional).

The useful side of the Controlling State allows you to respond to a wide variety of repetitive situations without thinking them through over and over (again, not emotional). This saves time and money in business and is seen as a strong trait among leaders.

The destructive side of the Controlling State is characterized by aggression, speaking in a loud voice, pointing and shaking your finger, ultimatums, scowls, and folded arms. This state is developed from a young age when the child either got his/her way by behaving in the Controlling State or observed a parent who behaved this way. The tendency to get into the Controlling State comes with a need to have things your own way and to control others. If a Controlling State person is dealing with a Immature State person, she is in her glory achieving what she wants by intimidation and control. If two Controlling State people are communicating together, you would hear a lot of shouting and arguing, possibly with no solution achieved.

Example: An extreme example of the destructive side of the Controlling State was demonstrated in a "How to Give Feedback" seminar. As Bill walked in to the room, it was evident that he was in the Controlling State and "on automatic control." Hostile body language, booming voice, accusing, extreme questioning, causing others to feel uncomfortable with his confrontational style, and becoming defensive when approached: these were the unmistable signs.

You may be thinking, *Is there any hope for Bill or someone like him?* Yes. It will take time and effort. This behavior can be turned down like the knob on your stove and replaced with more appropriate behavior, like the Freedom State. It is difficult to change behavior unless the person has a desire to do so or understands that this communication state is self-destructive in the work environment.

Your goal should be to stay out of the destructive Immature State and the Controlling State except on rare occasions: for example, the Immature State should be used in a situation where any other behavior may put you in physical danger. It is difficult to find a really good time to use the Controlling State, but sometimes it can be used as a shock tactic, especially if you are not known for behaving in this way.

The Freedom State.

This is the perfect communication state. It is a state that does not react to any type of difficult behavior, whether aggressive, passive, or argumentative. The characteristics are good eye contact at all times and self-confident body language—standing tall, holding your head straight, speaking in a clear voice, and unfolded arms. A strong feeling of confidence is the hallmark. This state is learned through constant practice. No matter what difficulty comes to you, your response in the Freedom State is not reactive. In the Freedom State your communication is based on fact; you do not judge. The Freedom State is the process by which you arrive at decisions, not the decisions themselves. The person who is the best at processing thoughts by using the Freedom State will have the best potential for success in all situations, especially business. Here are a few examples of how you would respond to difficult people by staying in the Freedom State:

> *Controlling State person (yelling):* "How could you have done such a stupid thing, you idiot!"
> *Freedom State response (standing straight, calm, making eye contact):* "Excuse me, do you have something to say to me?"
> *Controlling State person:* "Can't you hear? Are you stupid?"
> *Freedom State response:* "I would be glad to discuss your problem, but I can't help you when you are speaking to me in this manner."

If this type of abuse were to continue, the Freedom State person would leave, stating that the Controlling State person should return when he was ready to communicate in a reasonable manner. The Freedom State does not rise to the occasion by escalating into the Controlling State or back away by going into the Immature State. He stays strong and steadfast. Asking questions but not taking abuse. **He can be offended but not take offense.**

The person communicating in the Freedom State may initially cause a person in the Controlling State to become angry. He may raise his voice even more than before. When you stay in the Freedom State, it will eventually bring the Controlling State person to your level of calmness and sanity. He must change when he can not affect you as the has in the past.

What if you have to deal with someone who is whining, passive, or crying? Again in the Freedom State, dealing with only the facts, not emotional, you stay centered with good eye contact, a look of concern on your face but not overly sympathetic. Here is a sample conversation:

Immature State person (possibly crying and nervous): "I just don't know what to do, nothing is going right, everyone is out to get me, they are unfair by giving me so much work. . . .

Freedom State response (having placed the tissues in reach of the Immature State person and listening with a matter-of-fact attitude): "I see you are very upset. Do you need a few minutes to regain your composure or would you like to continue?"

Immature State person: "No, I'll be okay." *(more tears).*

Freedom State response: "Break down your problems one by one and come up with a possible solution for each. When you have done this, we'll discuss how you can improve your situation."

In the Freedom State, you do not become responsible for the problems of others. You listen with empathy, not sympathy, and direct them toward their own solution.

Next time you are in a difficult situation, watch your response. Did you go to the top of the scale, the destructive Controlling State, by raising your voice, accusing, or losing your composure? Or did you go to the lower end of the scale, the destructive Immature State, by withdrawing and feeling like a victim? If your response was either, begin to practice responding to the facts, staying calm and focused, using your best option, the Freedom State.

BEHAVIOR TRAITS OF THE THREE STATES

IMMATURE STATE	FREEDOM STATE	CONTROLLING STATE
Destructive Traits *Emotional Response*	*Factual Response*	*Destructive Traits* *Reactive Response*
passive	open	aggressive
fearful	eye contact	glaring or staring
tearful	calm	agitated
withdrawn	strong voice	loud
wringing hands	confident	pointing finger
poor eye contact	good listener	crossed arms
looking away	concern	poor listener
low voice	asks questions	demands
nonconfrontational	nonjudgmental	confrontational

CHAPTER FOUR

MANAGING YOUR PROBLEM EMPLOYEES

Have you ever felt like pulling your hair out because you, as a manager, just couldn't seem to get your problem employee to change? Perhaps he/she has a bad attitude, is negative, won't take responsibility, will only work "by the rules" instead of the "spirit of the rules," has a hundred excuses for every mistake, or just does not get to work on time. Any of these problems can take a tremendous amount of your managing time, add stress to your job, and lower morale in the business environment.

The answer for dealing with 98 percent of these problem employees is not a complex program that will take you hours to read and absorb, but then be easy to do once you understand it. It is actually a very simple process, so simple that you may want to discard it, but this is tough to do. Why? Because you will have to stop reacting to all the little rabbit trails (excuses) your employees want to take you down and learn to stay focused on the issue facing you.

How do you do this? Start managing the specific behavior that you need changed. You cannot manage attitudes or backgrounds or personal problems. No one can tell you how to do that. If you continue trying, you will become a full-time therapist, not a manager. You can only manage the behavior that comes out of those situations. When you observe an employee who has a poor attitude, ask yourself, What exactly is this person with the bad attitude doing? Is he or she answering the phone incorrectly? Is he or she arriving late to meetings? Is he or she talking negatively about a change that is occurring? When you can pinpoint the answer to this question, then manage that specific behavior.

Oprah Winfrey demonstrated a personal example of being direct while managing behavior on her October 26, 1994, show. This show was about the differences in communication styles—male, female; power position, subordinate position; direct, indirect. During the show Oprah expressed her stress regarding the slow repair of a clock that she had given to an employee who was responsible for this type of repair. It had been weeks since the initial request, but her clock was still in repair and she had not received a replacement. She really needed a clock. Her technique was to ask daily in a rather indirect way, nice, not urgent, and focused on the convenience of the maintenance man. Oprah said, Wait a minute, I need to be more direct and she promptly called for this man to come on the set so that she could ask directly for what she wanted, a clock. He arrived to be seen by millions, and Oprah said directly, "I need a clock immediately because without a clock I am late." He was so nice and said he would try. It would have been very easy to accept the "I'll try" answer but "I'll try" does not guarantee the result you need.

Oprah took on the body language of understanding and warmth, putting her arm around him, tipping her head, but stayed direct in her request while repeating it two or three times. She finally got a commitment that he would get her a clock. Within seven minutes he arrived back at the set with two clocks for her to choose from. Oprah was thrilled. This example may look easy because the man had to go on national television, and it seems natural that he would want to do what his boss requested. Granted this is a unique situation but no easier or harder to resolve than any other situation. First, the maintenance man was so nice that Oprah may have found it hard to be direct without feeling that she was being insensitive. Second, he gave the "I'll try" answer we all get so often. He had already tried, and Oprah was still without a clock. Remember "I'll try" can mean there is no real commitment to achieve the goal.

Part of managing behavior requires that you stop attempting to fix all the employee's reasons for not doing what he or she was hired to do. It is clear that erasing these excuses will not help the employee change; he or she will just come up with more excuses. What it will accomplish is take the responsibility away from the employee and put it directly on the manager's shoulders. You will have more unwanted work. Now you will be playing Mommy or Daddy. If there is a change, you will have to continue the role of Mommy or Daddy at all times to guarantee that the change continues.

*Excuses and explanations: An excuse is using an explanation about why we did something to avoid responsibility for paying the consequences. An explanation simply explains our thoughts, feelings, and actions and keeps us responsible.**

Most managers are not trained in the area of managing behavior. They are told what they should do but not how to do it. They are promoted to a job because their past record has been excellent, and it is assumed that the "people managing skills" are just a

---

*Lynn Seiser, MA, MFCC, newsletter, April 1994.

natural step in their progress that they can achieve through experience. Many managers-in-training (pre-manager position) have experienced role models who used the stick method—"You do it or else"—or their role model did not have any significant management style that was effective in changing behavior. Therefore, as new managers, or not-so-new managers, they just keep perpetuating the same problems.

Changing to a new method of management is not comfortable for anyone, but if the outcome is an improvement in performance, then the price is well worth the pain. Remember, if you keep doing what you have always done, you will keep getting what you have always gotten.

It is fairly easy to manage an employee that you like or has a style similar to your own. The employees who are stressful to manage are the ones you do not like or who are different from you. These employees are the small percentage you deal with. The law of 80/20, which states that you spend 80 percent of your time on 20 percent of your employees (the problem employees), is the focus of this chapter. The following model will work in all situations whether it is a casual meeting in the hall, a sit-down counseling session, or a union warning session.

1. Describe the specific behavior you want changed.

Example: "Don, I am talking with you this morning to discuss your work schedule. You were 10 minutes late on Monday, 15 minutes on Tuesday, and 5 minutes today."

Begin your conversation with the behavior you want changed. Do not begin with a compliment or positive reinforcement. Many training models encourage you to build the employee up at the beginning of a corrective feedback session. DON'T. Why? First, because the employee will come to expect that when something good is said, the next words out of your mouth will

cause the other shoe to drop. Second, because the positive reinforcement is lost in the conversation. Save the positive statement
for the end of the conversation or keep it totally separate. Help the
employee to feel okay when he or she leaves the feedback session so
the needed change can occur. *Remember, any statement preceding the
word "but" is erased.* If you want to change behavior, plan and prepare to give very specific information regarding the behavior, stating time, date, or a description of exactly what has occurred. Do
not generalize.

2. Tell why the behavior is ineffective in the work environ-
ment.

Example: "Don, this is ineffective because it is disruptive to our
morning meetings. I need to repeat the information you missed,
and arriving late sends a message to the other employees that
promptness is not important."

Telling why the behavior is ineffective helps to stop excuses,
or denials. It is another step in making the employee take responsibility for the outcome of his/her behavior.

3. Pause and wait for the employee's response.

Example: Silence . . . Dons' response: "You know I drive a long
distance and that traffic is unpredictable. Plus I always get my work
done. . . . It feels like you are just picking on me."

A pause, or a silence, is used instead of a question asking for
the excuses or reasons. When you pause, it allows the employee to
take the information you have stated, think about it, and then respond. If you ask a question, the employee only needs to answer the
question and can disregard all previous information. Silence can
feel uncomfortable. Stay silent anyway. Do not feel the need to fill

the empty space with more explanations. Put the responsibility where it belongs, on the employee.

A common question that I am asked is: "What if he just sits there and does not say anything?" Rarely will this happen. The employee will usually feel the need to break the silence. If it does continue past a normal pause (approximately 45 seconds), then your response should be, "Your silence tells me you understand and agree with my observations." Then go directly immediately to Step 5.

4. Acknowledge the employee's response without going off track (down any of those rabbit trails).

Example: "I am sorry you feel picked on and I understand the traffic situation, however . . ." Go on to Step 5.

This acknowledgment step tends to be the moment of truth. Can you stay focused or will you begin to solve all of your employee's problems. A statement that a seminar participant used seems very appropriate at this moment, just say to yourself, "DON'T GO THERE."

5. State what needs to be changed or stopped.

Example: "Don, you must be here every morning at 8 A.M."
Be clear, concise, and confident. Know exactly what you need changed or stopped.

6. Ask the employee how she or he will make this change.

Example: "How, will you get here every morning at 8 considering the traffic?"

Some managers tell me, "I don't care how, I just want them to do it." Asking **how,** again, puts the responsibility back on the employee. The employee must come up with a way in his or her mind to achieve the changes needed. "I'll try" does not imply a change. He or she is probably trying already and not achieving the goals. Once you get the how, you still only manage the final behavior expected. It is the employee's responsibility to take care of the how.

7. Receive a commitment from your employee and repeat it back to her or him.

Example: Don: "Well, I guess I could leave 15 minutes earlier."
Manager: "Good, do I hear you correct? You are making a commitment to leave home 15 minutes earlier every morning so you will be here on time?"
Don: "Yes." . . . Go to step 9.

Whatever the employee says is his or her commitment. The words need to come out of the employee's mouth. It really does not matter if his or her "how" is different from yours as long as the needed change is accomplished.

8. Give natural consequences if the commitment cannot be met.

Example: After the manager has asked approximately three times for the "how," Don still will not commit and he replies: "I can't guarantee that the traffic will not make me late, I have no control over the traffic."
Manager: "Don, since you do not have a way you see to change this situation, I will have to put you on suspension the next time you are late. Do you understand?"

Natural consequences only are given when the employee will not come up with a way to change.

9. Set a time to review the situation and evaluate if the commitment is being met.

Example: "Don, I'll check with you in a week to see how you are doing."

An evaluation time with a followup must occur. Manager, whatever you say you will do, write it on your calendar and then do it.

10. Affirm the employee's ability to make the change and end on a positive note.

Example: "I know you can do this, Don. Your sales this quarter are in the top 10 percent and I feel really good about having you on the team. Thank you."

Leave the employee with confidence and a desire to improve. The only exception to ending on a positive note is when the natural consequences (Step 8) must be given.

In the role plays with hundreds of managers, the positive note at the end is forgotten many times. Finishing and getting out of the uncomfortable situation is the main desire and focus of most managers. However, you should slow down, think, and remember that if the employee feels good about her- or himself in one area, she or he will be much more likely to change her or his behavior in another area.

The following is an actual example of a role play done by a manager and a employee. The excuse the employee gave scores high on the list of *how to get my boss off track so I do not have to take responsibility.* Read how this manager handled her employee with ease and confidence using the model.

   Manager: "Steve, I have called you into my office to discuss the way you answer the phone. As we have discussed in the past, you are only saying hello. The company policy is you must say your name and your department."

Steve attempts to interrupt but the manager asks him to wait just a minute until she is finished and says that then she will listen.

Manager (continuing): "This is ineffective because the customer will not know for sure if he is talking to the correct department and could also slow down any return calls because the customer would not have a name to refer to for problems."

Steve: "Perhaps you do not know, but I cannot use my name because I'm hiding from my ex-wife. This is why I just say hello."

At this point most managers would react to this statement by discounting it, or accusing the employee of being untruthful, or just being at a loss for words.

Manager (no visual reaction): "Steve, it does not matter what name you use as long as you use it consistently. You must say a name and your department when answering all calls. How will you do that?"

Steve: "I don't know."

Manager: "That distresses me." *Manager repeats her request one more time.*

Steve: "So I guess I can use 'Don'—that's my brother's name."

Manager: "Do I understand that you have commited to answer all calls consistently by saying your department and the name you have chosen?"

Steve: "Yes."

Manager: "Good. I will check back with you in one week to see how the calls are proceeding. I know this will be a help for all concerned. By the way, I want to compliment you on the way your followup paperwork has been done. It is always clear and concise and I appreciate it."

As a manager, you can never be sure what your employee is thinking or what reason or excuse he or she will give you for not performing the required job. When you step out of your own emotional, reactive way, think . . . be prepared . . . use the model . . . stay calm . . . and respond (not react), you will be able to achieve the behavior change in 98 percent of your problem employees.

Are you wondering about the other 2 percent? This model will not work with drug, or alcohol abuse, or mental illness. Employees with these types of problems need special help, but a kind referral by the manager to a professional can be helpful. Hopefully they will choose to get the help they need.

CHAPTER FIVE

HOSTILE-AGGRESSIVE BEHAVIOR PROBLEMS

Hostile-aggressive behavior is probably the most difficult for a manager or co-employee to deal with. Whatever form it comes in its underlying antagonism can make even the strongest person run for cover. Some of the terms and characteristics used to describe hostile-aggressive behavior by seminar attendees are: aggressive, calling people unmentionable names, playing points-scoring and justification games, rudeness, throwing tantrums, sarcasm, back-stabbing comments, causing conflict in any way possible.

Hostile-aggressives can appear out of control at times, but don't be fooled, such people usually know exactly what they are doing. If you show any signs of weakness, you may leave yourself open to attack and possibly become their prey. Their behavior says,

"I want it my way, right now, regardless of your needs."

The more you react to a hostile-aggressive's behavior, the less influence you will have over the situation. Before spending any time getting frustrated about this type of person, ask yourself, What can I actually influence? What is out of my control. Now, respond to what you can influence and leave what is out of your control alone.

There are seven basic strategies for dealing with Hostile-Aggressives:
1. Let their steam run out.
2. Don't take their abuse; leave if need be.
3. Get help when you need it.
4. Don't laugh at them.
5. Show your disapproval.
6. Change what they say to something more acceptable and repeat it back.
7. Only respond to what you can influence.

And read on, there is more help!

• EXPLOSIVES—HOW TO RECOGNIZE THE SYMPTOMS AND AVOID BEING THE TARGET

David, whom I mentioned at the beginning of Chapter 2, is an example of the Explosive. He was very clear that his aggressive style of behavior got him what he wanted. He used it on the phone with secretaries to reach the people he wanted to talk to. The secretaries certainly did not want to deal with him; therefore they would do whatever he wanted. He behaved in this manner with anyone who was beneath him in status or anyone who needed his business.

Explosives become out of control, often without any warning. They are loud, slamming a book on the table or shaking a finger while yelling at you. They use accusatory, name-calling techniques such as "You idiot!" or "How could you be so stupid?" They interrupt you to tell you how wrong your point of view is: "Only an idiot would think that way."

When dealing with an Explosive, you feel as if you can't say anything without causing more abuse. You feel you want to hide. Explosives reduce many people to tears. They can and do make others appear out of control by taking charge of the situation by force.

Explosives have learned this behavior and perfected it because it works to accomplish what they want, at least at that particular moment. Often you will find these people in a position of authority, which adds to your fear of communicating with them.

If you seem to be a victim of this type of behavior, examine what makes you an easy target. Ask yourself the following questions:

1. Are you timid, using a faint, soft voice?

2. Do you feel unsure of yourself?

3. Do you lack confidence that the information you are discussing is correct and up to date?

4. Are you inexperienced, or new to the job?

5. Do you have low self-esteem?

6. Do you put up with this behavior hoping that it will stop or go away?

7. Do you disregard your own feelings?

If you answered yes to any of these questions, the first step is to change those traits that make you an easy target. If your voice is weak, record it and listen to it, then start working on it until you can hear a definite improvement. End your sentences with a downward tone when making a strong statement, an upward one for a question. You can also take singing lessons in order to learn to speak from your diaphragm for a fuller voice. It is a proven fact that the lower and clearer your voice the more power you are perceived to have.

If you are feeling unsure of yourself, the best thing to do is to remain silent until you are confident about what you have to say. An adage I like is: If you have nothing to say, don't let anyone persuade you to say it.

Are you new to the job? Inexperienced? Once you know that there is an Explosive to deal with, make every attempt to stay out of his way until you have more experience. Don't act like an expert before you are one.

Low self-esteem is something many people suffer from. I often hear the statement: "He makes me feel bad/lowers my self-esteem." Remember: **No one makes us have low self-esteem.** It is an inside job, something we do to ourselves through years of self-abuse and poor self-talk. Begin by being more positive about yourself. Do not put yourself down using phrases like "I was so stupid," "This is a dumb question," or "I'm sorry." Begin by telling yourself that you are smart, useful, correct: now add two adjectives of your own. Remember, **You are what you say you are all day long!**

If your self-esteem is high and none of the personal issues above apply to you, maybe you have put up with the Explosive's behavior because you didn't know how to deal with it. There will be no more reasons to be a victim if you follow these basic strategies for dealing with the Explosive:

    1. Don't use fighting words like "You're wrong."
       You can never win a fight with an Explosive. Do

say things like "In my opinion . . ." or "I don't agree with you but I want to hear more of what you're saying."

2. Use the Explosive's name at the beginning of the conversation or whenever you want to take control.

3. Keep eye contact at all times. You will appear more in control of yourself. When you look away, it appears that you are weak or afraid, and the Explosive will know he has his next victim.

4. Don't tell him about your weakness, whatever it is: he will not have sympathy and will only point it out to you at every chance he gets.

5. Let him explode until he has run out of powder. Once that happens and you begin to speak he may interrupt you.

6. Stop the Explosive from interrupting you by telling him "You interrupted me," then continue with what you were saying. Each time he interrupts, you must stop him with the same sentence, "You interrupted me." If you allow him to continue interrupting, he will see you as weak again and your point of view will never be heard.

7. Don't take his attacks personally. An Explosive would say the same thing to anyone who was available.

8. Make sure that your communication is at eye level, either sitting or standing. Don't stay seated when he is standing over you.

Once you have dealt appropriately with the Explosive, he will have a new respect for you. You will find him coming to you with questions and information that you never thought he would share with you. Remember, though, that he is an Explosive, and if he reverts to his old ways, you must return to the same solution behavior.

SITUATION 1. My supervisor has a lousy management style. I find it hard to work for her, but I always do my best. She comes across as bossy, pushy, almost like a slave-driver. I think she is that way so that she can impress her boss (the V.P.) who will see her as a capable manager, able to get "the teams" working to their full potential. I think she is just a bitch! *Jane.*

I am sure that Jane always does her best. But is it good enough to keep her sane, self-confident, and basically happy? There are some basic things that she can do to feel good about herself: this is most important, since her manager may never change. At the same time, she needs tools to build a better work relationship.

First of all, Jane should not take her superior's attitude personally. It is probably true that the manager wants to impress her boss. Perhaps Jane should ask how she can help her achieve this goal. It may be against her nature, but it is one solution to the problem. If you want to tell someone how you feel, speak in "I" sentences instead of "you" sentences—for example: "I find it difficult to feel competent about my work when I have projects on my desk without time for clear communication. When would be a good time to review these items?" Stay in the "how I feel" mode instead of the "you did it to me" mode. Ask questions that cannot be answered with simply "yes" or "no"—for example: "Project A is due at 5 P.M. and I have just received this rush request from Mr. Z. Would you rather postpone Project A until tomorrow, or shall I delegate it to Miss X?"

Jane should put herself in her manager's place, even if that feels uncomfortable, and see how she will hear and accept what it is that Jane wants to get across. (Review the exercise in Chapter 2.) Acting out situations with a friend or spouse helps. If there is no one to act out with, then talk out loud by yourself and play both parts. Acting out is a form of rehearsing what you want to say. Do not expect to feel and act confident without practice.

> **Note: Every situation we find ourselves in is an opportunity for growth.**

SITUATION 2. I have a difficult staff member, Don, who has worked in the same position for about six years. He has recently become extremely aggressive to his fellow workers, and I have been put in charge of him to correct the situation. Senior management have advised me not to move him yet. I feel that I need some new skills in order to handle this situation. *Fred.*

In this situation, I would advise Fred to call Don into his office and talk in a nonattacking warm tone, regardless of Don's initial response. It is important that Fred stays in the Freedom State. He could start by asking questions—for example: "I have noticed that you're not as happy and calm as you used to be." Give Don some examples of the behavior; otherwise this is only an opinion not a fact. "Don, a week ago I observed you yelling at Bill because he could not help you quickly enough, three days ago you slammed Mary's office door when you left, and just today you totally ignored June when she was asking you a question. You have always been calm in the past, what has changed? Are there some problems that are affecting you?" If, after these questions, Don still will not open up, then Fred might say, "Don, have a guess at why things have changed, just make it up, anything." At this point Don may try to make light of the situation and say something sarcastic, such as "Everyone hates me," "Everyone but me gets a promotion," or something similar. Whatever Don says, Fred should listen carefully, because this will be his clue. After Don has spoken, Fred should pause and not react immediately. Then he should come back with a serious response. No matter how strange Don's statement was, act as if it were the truth. If Don didn't give the real reason for his behavior, his response now may be, "Are you crazy, it's not that, it's . . ."

Points to remember when dealing with an Explosive:

Develop a strong voice for authority.

Remain silent.

Improve your self-talk.

Do not use fighting words.

Use the Explosive's name.

Keep eye contact.

Let the Explosive run out of steam.

Keep your weaknesses to yourself.

Stop the Explosive from interrupting.

Don't take things personally.

· INSULTING ATTACKERS—HOW YOU CAN PROTECT YOURSELF WHILE KEEPING YOUR SELF-ESTEEM

The verbal attack is a particularly difficult kind of "hook." The attacker's object is to get the victim emotionally involved in a no-win situation. When the attack is successful, the attacker feels superior to his victim.

There are many varieties of verbal attack, but the most common uses a negative presumption to hook the victim. Here are some examples, together with responses to keep you from becoming a victim:

Attack: "Any fool knows that this is the wrong way to report these numbers." (Presumes the victim is a fool.)
Response: "I'm sorry you feel I'm foolish. How would you like the numbers reported?"

Attack: "If you cared about this company, you wouldn't complain about this policy." (Presumes the victim doesn't care about the company.)
Response: "Of course I care about the company. Here's the problem with the policy . . ."

Attack: "If the personnel department would come down from its ivory tower, it would know that the employee leave policy is totally unworkable." (Presumes that the department isn't in touch.)
Response: "When did you start thinking that the personnel department is out of touch with reality?" (Don't ask *why*.)
Attack: "You're not the only person in this department, you know. Everyone thinks Bill lets you get away with murder." (Presumes the victim is devious.)
Response: "Of course I'm not the only person in the department." (Then change the subject.)

Remember: "The basic strategy for the verbal attack is to respond to the presumption, not the accusation or insult."★
People who use insulting attacks often don't have very high self-esteem, so they use their attacks to build themselves up. When you respond by defending yourself or being hostile, you become

---

★*Success with the Gentle Art of Verbal Self-Defense,* Suzette Hadden Elgin's cassette album.

part of the game. This only encourages it to continue. Follow these basic strategies when dealing with Insulting Attackers:

1. Only respond to the actual facts of the situation.

2. Stay calm. Never respond with hostility.

3. Think about why this person needs to put you down. Once you can understand his underlying reasons, you will be able to respond in a more productive manner. This doesn't mean that you will like his behavior, but if you do understand it and continue to stay calm, it is quite possible that he will begin to change.

4. Ask questions: "Why would you say that?" or "Could you explain?"

5. Leave the situation.

6. Let the Insulting Attacker know you will not be a victim of his or her attacks.

7. Watch your body language. Keep eye contact and show self-confidence.

8. Don't get hooked by acting on your anger.

SITUATION 3. I regularly visit customers who are very irate because of service failures. I have to listen and not take their verbal abuse personally while resolving the problem. *Mary.*

There are a number of issues here: the customers' behavior, the problem (or customer service failure) and Mary's feelings. If one responds to the problem directly, it will take a lot of the steam out of the customer's anger. Mary should reassure the customers that she is resolving their problems as she has done for them in the past.

The biggest issue is how to not feel abused. The childhood saying, "Sticks and stones may break my bones but names will never hurt me," is incorrect. Feeling upset, hurt, anger or rage is normal. Feelings are facts, too. Try not to act on them. Don't hold your breath when you are being attacked: this will only add to your stress. Breathe and tell yourself, "This is not about me." Anyone who happened to be there would get the same treatment. You could actually say, "I know you are not angry with me but that you are very upset about this problem: let me show you how I intend to solve it." When you leave, take a few minutes to get the situation out of your system. The quicker you calm down the less of an effect these verbal attacks will have on you, physically and mentally.

SITUATION 4. During a meeting, an individual evades the point and reacts with personal attacks. These attacks have a disruptive influence on the whole meeting. *Peter.*

Peter can respond in a number of different ways. First, he should not react to the personal attacks. He should maintain strong eye contact when these remarks are made, but he should not comment—merely repeat the question. If he continually refuses to respond, the attacker will not know what to do. Peter is not playing his game and he will have to go elsewhere.

Second, Peter can bring out his hidden agenda by saying, "That was a hurtful remark. Please tell me why you said that." He should question the attacker as long as he needs to in order to get at the undercover anger or hidden agenda.

Third, Peter can go back to the basic strategy of responding to the presumption not the attack, as stated earlier in this section.

Points to remember when dealing with an Insulting Attacker:

Don't get hooked by the Insulting Attacker.

Respond to the presumptions, not to the insults.

Stay calm.

Understand the Insulting Attacker's need to build
   himself up at your expense.

Stay out of the game.

Don't act on your own anger.

Keep eye contact.

Bring out the hidden agenda of the Insulting Attacker.

Stay in the Freedom State.

• HIDDEN SARCASM—LEARN TO RECOGNIZE HURTFUL SARCASM IMMEDIATELY AND RESPOND (NOT REACT) TO KEEP IT OUT IN THE OPEN AND AWAY FROM YOU

Most people fall for this type of behavior more than once in their lives. The common response from a victim is to act as if nothing hurtful, negative, or sarcastic has been said to them. If this happens to you, you may even laugh or smile at the attacker. When it is over you feel furious and confused at why you didn't respond immediately. "How could I let them talk to me that way?" is a common reaction after this type of attack. If you do respond at the time, the attacker will say, "Oh, I was just joking. Don't be so sensitive."

You need to bring the sarcasm out into the open with an appropriate response. If the sarcasm is hidden in humor, you can say, "I enjoy laughing too, but that felt like a put-down. Was it?" You should expect a denial that it was a put-down. You can then respond with: "Okay, I just wanted to be sure, because it didn't feel very funny to me." With this type of probing, the attacker will begin, at least, to direct his sarcasm elsewhere. This tactic should be used in a one-to-one situation, but if you have no other choice, then do it in public.

Here are several basic strategies for dealing with Hidden Sarcasm:

1. Bring the sarcasm out into the open.

2. Question for intent.

3. Don't act vulnerable.

4. Find out the hidden agenda. Is the attacker jealous or angry?

5. Respond only to the compliment part of the sarcasm, not the put-down.

6. Realize that this person is not going to change. Do not give him the benefit of the doubt.

The key to dealing successfully with Hidden Sarcasm is to avoid the trap. If you are drawn into participating in the game, you generally lose. You'll know you have been trapped if:

You say something in anger you later regret.

You are boiling inside at what the attacker said or did.

Your response is uncharacteristic behavior for you.

You can avoid the trap by recognizing it. Refuse to get involved. Remember, no one can trap you without your participation. Decide which technique will work for you, and then do it. Preparation will help tremendously, but sometimes the trap is a total surprise. When this happens, stop and take a few seconds to remind yourself, *I am in control of my response. What do I want to say?* Use self-talk to validate who you are—for example, "I have the perfect answer" or "This person will not get to me."

SITUATION 5. Continual comparison with a co-worker or colleague, one who makes me feel less than equal—for example, "But X does it this way and she always gets it finished before she leaves." This person always acts nice when he is saying these things and it makes it hard to respond. What can I do that will help and not make me look as if I am too sensitive. *Nicki.*

Nicki should calmly ask, "Did you have a criticism of my work you wanted to discuss?" If he responds that he didn't mean anything, then she should tell him that it sounded as if he did, and that she is available for discussion if he has a problem. She must keep her voice confident, light, and not attacking.

SITUATION 6. A line manager is very sneaky. She never takes a stance. She waits to see who will win, then takes that position and talks about everyone else. She hates being challenged. *Alex.*

Even though this situation is a bit convoluted, it is still a form of Hidden Sarcasm. It is not surprising that the manager hates being challenged. She is using indirect aggression. She does not have the confidence to take a position that may not be popular. She is also building herself up at the expense of others. It is obvious that low self-esteem is her problem.

We now know the manager's problem, but how does that help Alex to deal with *his* problem—the manager? Understanding her way of thinking and her lack of confidence will help Alex in his solution. It is important that Alex does not take part in any of the negative conversations about other people. Equally, he should not ignore the comments either, as this is silent support. He should stop the manager by saying, "I respect whatever decisions others make, regardless of my choices. Thanks, but I don't want to talk about them." If Alex finds that this woman is talking about *him,* then he should approach her with "Did you have a criticism you wished to discuss with me?" When she says "no" (remember she hates confrontation), Alex can respond with, "Oh, then I must have been confused by your comments. I just want you to know you can talk to me directly if there is any problem."

This won't change her need to hide and be safe, but Alex can feel better about how he is dealing with it and protecting himself.

SITUATION 7. A friend of mine is always putting me down. When I can't stand it any more, I stop seeing her. When we get together again she is fine for a while, but it always starts up again. I feel so angry that I allow it but I can never think of the right thing to say at the time, so I just stop seeing her again. Sometimes I'll tell her something, a concern or worry, and then she uses it against me but always with the illusion of being nice. *Carolyn*.

It is good for Carolyn to stop seeing her friend, but it will be even better when she can stop the put-downs. As in the last situation, this is happening because of the friend's own problems, but that doesn't make it feel any better. Let's look at why Carolyn allows it. She should evaluate her own fears about speaking out. How important is it for her to be liked? Is she afraid of losing her temper? Or is it just that she needs the correct tools to deal with the situation.

Next time this friend makes a put-down statement, Carolyn should stop her immediately and say, "That felt like a put-down, could you explain exactly what you meant?" If she responds that Carolyn is being too sensitive, Carolyn should say, "I want to be your friend but I need you to hear me, and, by the way, that last statement felt like a put-down as well." If she really wants Carolyn as a friend, this could be the beginning of a true relationship. If not, Carolyn will have learned the skills she needs to stop being a victim.

Points to remember when dealing with Hidden Sarcasm:

Don't laugh at sarcasm hidden in humor.

Bring sarcasm out in the open.

Don't believe that the behavior will change.

Be prepared.

Let the attacker know that you don't appreciate his or her comments.

Don't take part in sarcasm directed at someone else.

Speak up; don't give silent support.

Look at your own fear of speaking up.

Ask the attacker to explain his or her comments.

CHAPTER SIX

PASSIVE-AGGRESSIVE
BEHAVIOR PROBLEMS

We often think of aggressive behavior as being character-ized by defiance or resistance. This can be the case, as we have discussed in previous chapters, but often aggression is hidden and passive. Passive-aggressive personalities have a hidden agenda that is not as easy to recognize as simple aggressive behavior. Such a person might seem very concerned about you, while all the time he or she is really gathering material with which to undermine your authority.

Passive-Aggressives can avoid the most confrontational situations through manipulation. They do not like to take responsibility because this may put them at risk of failure.

Passive-Aggressives may also tell you whatever they think you want to hear, just to keep you happy and off their backs. You will discover this by watching what they do, not by listening to what they say. A productive approach to the Passive-Aggressive is "Don't tell me, just show me."

Some of the characteristics of a Passive-Aggressive person are:

1. Fear over lack of control of his life.

2. Feeling that he is controlled by others.

3. Low self-esteem.

4. Fear of failure.

5. Self-deprecation and difficulty in accepting compliments.

6. Indifference, feeling that nobody will listen anyway.

7. Respect for others but not him- or herself.

8. Allowing others to choose for him or her.

In this chapter we will discuss three types of Passive-Aggressive behavior: Silent Judges, Avoiders, and Information-Keepers.

• SILENT JUDGES—HOW TO TURN UNRESPONSIVE BEHAVIOR INTO OPEN COMMUNICATION

Silent Judges are the people who do not respond when you ask them a question. They do not acknowledge your conversation with the usual "uh huh" or "yes, I understand" or "tell me more" type of answers. If you have a Silent Judge on the phone, you may think they have gone to sleep because of the lack of response. Silent Judges are so named because it can feel as if they are judging you even when they may not be. Their silence can be irritating, frustrating, confusing, and upsetting. It seems almost impossible to figure out why they are being silent. Are they judging you, angry, confused, trying to sabotage you, or just plain shy?

Many people who use silence do so as a means of aggression. They are aware that it frustrates you and can even make you angry. People who use silence use it intentionally because it gets them what they want. There is a saying in sales: "He who speaks first loses." This often works because when the buyer has a desire to own the item and the seller remains silent, the buyer will usually talk himself into the sale.

Here are some basic strategies for dealing with Silent Judges:

1. The most important thing for you to do when dealing with the Silent Judge is to get him to talk.

2. Watch his or her body language in order to get some feedback on how he or she is feeling. For example:

   ·If his arms are crossed tightly over his chest and he has a frown on his face, he is probably hostile.
   ·If she has her hands clasped low in front of her or behind her back and is looking down, she may be feeling insecure.
   ·If he is tapping his foot or fingers, he is saying, "You are wasting my time."
   ·If she is ignoring you by looking at the ceiling or out of the window, she is bored.

   Once you have observed his or her body language, you can begin to have a better idea of how to talk to him or to her.

3. Ask open-ended questions. These are questions that cannot be answered by a simple "yes" or "no" but require a statement—for example: "How do you feel about that?" "What is your opinion of this?" or "What is your reaction to this situation?"

4. You *must* be silent after asking a question or making a statement. Do not speak, no matter how long it takes the Silent Judge to respond to your question.

5. Take control of the silence. Don't look threatening by staring or frowning. Instead look inquisitive, eyes wide open.

6. When the Silent Judge does respond, allow the person to carry on the conversation as long as possible.

7. Do not interrupt. When you do speak again, support the communication by asking another pertinent open-ended question in order to keep him or her involved.

What if these strategies do not work? There need to be boundaries set for what you will and will not accept. The following situations demonstrate two different types of boundary:

1. You are the boss dealing with a silent subordinate. "John, we have not been able to talk about your constant late starts at work. I will have to make a note of this in your file, and if it continues, the only action I will be able to take is to let you go." This is a boundary of responsibility. The subordinate will have to take responsibility for his actions by either communicating or being fired.

2. You are the subordinate dealing with a silent boss. "Thank you, Ms. Jones, I assume that the lack of response means that you are pleased with the project and we have nothing else to discuss." Then stand up and begin to leave. This is a boundary of

time. If you cannot get communication going with the boss, you are showing that you will not spend a lot of time playing a silent game.

If you are in a family situation dealing with a silent partner, employ open-ended questions. Boundaries are more difficult to use without causing additional friction in the relationship. For example: "Darling, I have asked you about planning our holiday but have not had a response from you. Is there something bothering you about going away, or can we schedule an hour tonight to talk about it?" This is an open-ended question that will start communication of some type.

If the partner's response is "No, there is nothing bothering me" then reiterate the second part of the question: "Good, what time would you like to set aside to discuss our plans?"

Do not attack a silent partner. It will only cause him or her to become more withdrawn. An attack would sound like this: "You never discuss our holiday plans with me. Time is running out. I want to know what we're going to do! I certainly don't want to sit around like last year." These statements show anger and frustration and will not do anything to open up a silent person.

SITUATION 1. I have an employee who does things without checking to see if his actions are correct. He is secretive, deeply resents his work being checked or corrected, and will not respond when questioned. I am very stressed and don't know how to get him to talk to me. *Pamela.*

This employee appears to have strong fears about being wrong. His behavior is almost like that of a naughty child—secretive, resentful, and silent. Behaving like a parent, demanding, commanding, and critical, will only make the situation worse. Pamela should stay in the Freedom State: strong, unaffected by the emotions of others, stating the facts. She should confront her employee in a clear manner, without letting this man's behavior change her own. For example, imagine that Pamela is checking her employee's work and that the employee is reacting with resentment:

> *Pamela:* "You seem angry that I have evaluated your project." (This should be said in a calm and assertive way, not in a sympathetic manner. Stay silent after statement.)
>
> *Employee:* Remains silent, with hostile body language and some deep breaths showing exasperation.
>
> *Pamela:* "This won't change unless you can talk to me about your feelings." (This should be said in a matter-of-fact tone.)
>
> *Employee:* Grumbling, but no response.
>
> *Pamela:* "That's fine, I'll be back tomorrow to evaluate the next project. Let me know if you want to talk or need any help." (Pamela should now leave.)

Pamela should use this type of behavior continuously in order to let the employee see that she will not be affected by his attitude. It is not easy, but it will work if Pamela does not regress to anger, or commanding communication.

SITUATION 2. One employee refuses to talk to another even on a strictly performance basis. *Cheryl*

Solution: This is called in-fighting, and is similar to what children do in primary school (review the Immature State in Chapter 3). There are times when we are all children in grown-up bodies, and it may feel like a dirty trick. But the preference for this behavior would be during play, fun times not the professional work environment. It would be nice to think that we, as adults, have outgrown this immature behavior, but if it got us what we wanted as children, then we may still think it will get us what we want now.

I would advise Cheryl to meet with the non-communicator privately. She should give him the opportunity to air his hostilities, and then let him know that if he does not discuss the problem or behave in a more appropriate manner, there will be natural consequences. Let him know exactly what these consequences will be. Then Cheryl might call in coworkers of the non-communicator and discuss the issue with them, making them jointly responsible for behaving in a professional manner. She could schedule a weekly meeting with both until the communication level is acceptable and has maintained that level for a month or more. If this does not work, she should consider letting the non-communicator go.

SITUATION 3. My boss does not acknowledge me when I am talking to him. He just sits there and says nothing. I tend to fill in all the blank spaces with unnecessary comments that only make things worse. He does this with everyone, not just me. He also does it on the phone, and I feel like saying, "Hello, are you there?" *Margaret.*

Margaret's boss is manipulating her and everyone else who is affected by his silence. This is pretty easy to deal with: all Margaret needs to do is stay silent whenever she has completed a statement, question, or response. While she is waiting for his response, she should sit still and maintain eye contact. She must not fidget or shuffle papers. If the silence seems painfully long, she can look away as if bored, but no matter what she should not speak.

The telephone silence can be handled the same way. Margaret should ask her question, or make her statement, and then wait. Once she stops playing the game, the game will stop. Once this begins to work she can share it with others or just pass this chapter around the office.

Points to remember when dealing with Silent Judges:

Watch the Silent Judge's body language for clues to his feelings.

Get the person to talk.

Ask open-ended questions.

Stay silent after asking a question.

Do not interrupt when he or she speaks.

Set boundaries or consequences.

Do not attack a Silent Judge.

Use a matter-of-fact tone of voice.

Get comfortable with silence and don't fill in the blanks.

• AVOIDERS—HOW TO GET THEM TO FACE NECESSARY CONFRONTATIONS

Avoiders will run as far as they can to stay away from confrontation. They won't discuss, debate, or dispute issues.

They can be nice people but are poor team players and leaders. They won't take a side in any issue or say what they are thinking, for fear that they will be wrong. Most of the time they are very good at getting people to like them and forgive them.

Sometimes avoiders will overcommit because they are afraid of saying no and having a confrontation. In the long run, they cause more stress for everyone by overcommitting rather than saying no in the first place.

Avoiders rarely criticize others even if they are angry because they do not want to look as if they are out of control. They will do anything to get the approval of other people.

Try these basic strategies for dealing with Avoiders:

1. Schedule a short meeting and discuss directly that communication needs to change. Help the Avoider to tell you what is on his or her mind.

2. Be open, direct, and friendly while expressing your views.

3. Force the Avoider's response by asking open-ended questions.

4. Be clear about your expectations while being patient and reasonable.

5. Assign tasks and make the Avoider responsible for the completion and reporting of them. Help him or her through rough spots that he or she will not be willing to discuss by saying, "I know this is a difficult assignment. If you don't mind, I would like to give you my ideas about how to get started. Then you can decide what is best for you."

6. Let the Avoider know that making mistakes is natural and common. We learn from our mistakes and go forward to success. Then when the Avoider does make a mistake or a wrong decision, support him or her. Help the Avoider feel safe.

7. Give him or her an "I win and you win" solution option when there is a conflict. Give the person some of what he or she wants and take some of what you need. This will reinforce the idea that confrontation does not have to mean that someone loses.

SITUATION 4. I am trying to rebuild a relationship with a colleague or coworker who has fundamentally differing views/opinions from other employees but won't discuss them. I hope you can help, as the separation seems to get worse all the time and he is really a nice person! *Bill.*

How does Bill know that his coworker has differing views

from the others if he will not discuss them? Bill's response to this question was: "I guessed this was the problem because he avoids most contact, keeps to himself, and has a negative attitude, which he expresses through his body language."

First, Bill needs to make his coworker feel safe about the differences. He should schedule a meeting and discuss the changes he has observed. He could start by asking him if there are any personal problems involved—home, family, financial. Bill may be surprised to find that his coworker is under some external stress that has caused this changed behavior. If this is the problem, then Bill should do what he can to support his coworker in these areas, and make suggestions regarding improving work communication and discuss differences of opinion. It should be easier when the coworker is feeling understood.

If there are no home problems, then Bill will need to probe about his coworker's views in order to get at the core issues. Don't allow these questions to be brushed aside. Bill should focus on the cause, not the effect of his coworker's behavior. He should let him know it is important for both of them to rebuild the relationship.

> **Note:** To this point the solution is much more personal than the management style discussed in Chapter 4, the reason being that Bill wants to rebuild a relationship, not just change low performance with this coworker.

If nothing works up to this point, then, as a last resort, Bill would need to use the guidelines of Managing Behavior given in Chapter 4. He should let the coworker know that he requires all team members to participate equally, give him a time frame in which to solve the differences, and if this man does not wish to do this he will be placed elsewhere (natural consequences).

SITUATION 5. This is about an assistant who consistently fails to make decisions. He is losing the confidence of his subordinates. *Clifford.*

This assistant is afraid of making a mistake and this fear has turned him into an Avoider. Obviously his avoidance is a bigger problem than if he were actually to make a mistake, because he is losing the confidence of other employees.

Hopefully it isn't too late to help. Clifford should schedule a private meeting and ask the assistant to prepare for it by listing all his fears—however ridiculous they might sound—about making wrong decisions or failing. He should be told that the longer the list is, the better. As mentioned in Situation 4, it is important to get at the cause of the avoidance, rather than the effect. Clifford should be willing to look at company policy and attitudes about making mistakes, to ensure that the company is not part of the cause.

Next, Clifford might offer help in making a decision about some work issue, by going over pros and cons and possible outcomes. He should, however, make the assistant ultimately responsible. Clifford can help by giving examples to show that decision-making, whether it is a popular decision or not, is necessary for getting ahead in business. The following story is just such an example.

Sarah's main responsibility was to produce industry trade shows. Her company encouraged her to come up with new types of related shows in order to increase revenue. About two years after she began her job, Sarah came up with what she thought was a new and brilliant idea. She did the research, and with the company's blessing, set about producing this major event. To cut a long story short, the event was a failure. The attendance was disastrous and the lost revenue was tremendous. The show closed early and the exhibitors wanted their money back. At this point, Sarah was devastated and was considering resigning before she got fired. Sarah's boss, who was not known for his kindness, called Sarah into his office. She was sure she was going to be fired. Her boss knew how upset she was and proceeded to tell her a story to demonstrate how achieving success rarely comes without some failures. He told her he was proud of her attempt, and that he did not want her to stop creating but to learn from this experience. At the end of the year, Sarah received the largest pay rise she had ever had, based on the risk factor she was willing to take. Sarah confided that in years where she had made the company lots of money, her pay rises had been much smaller.

This true story shows how to reinforce the attitude of risk-taking instead of the attitude of fear of failure.

SITUATION 6. I have known and worked with John for twelve years. Four years ago I promoted him because I considered him ready for and capable of new responsibilities. I am very troubled because he will not accept the responsibility required or undertake any training to develop his skills. What can I do? *June.*

Four years of John digging his heels in sounds very frustrating. There is a possibility that he does not want this position or is jealous of June's management position. Here are some steps that June could take:

1. Ask why he is not accepting the responsibility.

2. Whoever is taking the responsibilities that are supposed to be John's must stop.

3. John must be allowed to fail by having no one to take up the slack.

4. Give him a choice of training courses and require him to pick which one he will attend.

5. At the end of the course, ask him for an overview of the training he has taken.

6. Give him boundaries, have expectations. Since June has known John for twelve years, the friendship could be getting in the way of a directive style of management.

Points to remember when dealing with Avoiders:

Be direct, open, and friendly.

State expectations.

Make the Avoider responsible.

Help him or her through rough spots.

Encourage mistakes.

Give "I win and you win" solutions.

Help the Avoider to feel safe.

Use probing questions.

Set boundaries.

Don't do the Avoider's work for him or her.

· INFORMATION-KEEPERS—HOW TO GET THE INFORMATION YOU NEED WITHOUT WASTING TIME

Information-Keepers are synonymous with time-wasters, at least where you are concerned. They will disappear just when you need to talk to them or respond with a "don't bother me" attitude. Sometimes it feels as if you have to plead with them to get what you want.

Keeping information is a power issue for some people. The

power comes from the fact that they know what you need to know and that gives them control. The longer they keep the information, the more powerful they feel. Keeping information can also be a sign of wanting acknowledgment. Acknowledgment is what Information-Keepers need in order to feel respected. Acknowledgment also keeps them from feeling that they are being used or taken for granted. If they do not receive this acknowledgment on a regular basis they will stop giving the information you need, and will probably sulk. There are a few cases where Information-Keepers are so busy and wrapped up in their own world that they just don't think about the importance of giving you what you need.

Try these strategies when dealing with Information-Keepers:

1. Be very clear with your requests. Vagueness will make it easy for the Information-Keeper to leave out just what you might need.

2. Outline your needs and explain the goal you want to reach.

3. Put your request for information in writing and date it.

4. Be careful not to hurt the Information-Keeper's feelings.

5. If you can't seem to get his or her attention, ask the Information-Keeper to acknowledge your findings. Act as if you think the information you have is the final solution unless he or she sees it differently or needs to fill in some questionable spaces. For example, "David, I have completed the information regarding the Smith account. Would you take a quick look at it to be sure I haven't left anything out?" Then you could add, "Last time you saved my neck and I really appreciated it!"

6. Acknowledge her brilliance for having the information you need: "Nancy, I can't believe you got that information so quickly. This will be perfect now. Thanks!"

7. Be willing to show your ignorance in his area of expertise: "Don, I am just so bad at figures, I don't know what I would do without your help."

8. Acknowledge his help in front of another person: "Susan, did I tell you about that information John gave me about the XYZ client? I know it was a main reason I closed the account."

Strategies 5, 6, 7, and 8 may seem extreme for some situations. Obviously, adjust them to suit your personality and the circumstances. The more outrageous these statements seem to you, the more you probably need to work at saying them! Why? Because it may be difficult for you to give compliments or to build up other people's egos, and you need to practice. If you're having major problems with information being withheld, be willing to look at yourself through the Information-Keeper's eyes (review the exercise in Chapter 2).

SITUATION 7. Trying to get a clear explanation of problems from a client and then obtaining the information necessary to alleviate or solve the problem from another colleague. Neither of them seems to want to give me the information that I must have. *Pat.*

Let's start with getting clear information from the client. He obviously does not like details, or is in a hurry. Pat should establish what type of personality he has (see Chapter 1). My guess is that he is a Bumper Sticker Communicator. She should ask short and to-the-point questions. For clarity, she should paraphrase back to the client what she thinks he means: "To make sure I understand what the problem is, let me repeat what I heard." If there is a misunderstanding, this will clear it up. She should remember to be brief.

Next, the colleague. Playing the middle man between client and colleague is difficult and frustrating. Pat will need to show plenty of sensitivity and must be careful not to appear demanding. She could put her requests for information in writing and hand them to her colleague. This will let him know that she wants to make it easy for him to give her the information to help the client. She should remember to acknowledge his help each time, making it clear that the information is needed for the client and that she appreciates the help.

SITUATION 8. Trying to get some information from people who really aren't interested in providing it. This makes my job take twice as long and sometimes causes my deadlines to be missed. *Heather.*

This case is very typical and could be solved by using strategies discussed previously. Here are some ways for Heather to get started. She should begin by checking her own attitude when she makes the requests. Is she only thinking about her own needs? She should be concerned about other people's time and feelings, and aware of their need for acknowledgment. She could say: "I know how busy you are, Steve, but I hope you will be able to help. I am desperate for the Collins account information and you are the only one who has the figures needed to complete the project." She must avoid making a lot of "I" or "me" statements and focus on the person with the information. They don't really care about her deadlines.

Heather should next establish what type of communicator the other person is (see Chapter 1). If he is a Technocratic Communicator, for example, he will not want to hear about any personal needs, and she should just talk facts. Technocratic Communicators don't usually want to be bothered by talkers.

Points to remember when dealing with Information-Keepers:

Be clear with your requests.

Outline needs.

Put requests in writing.

Don't hurt the Information-Keeper's feelings.

Ask for confirmation of your findings.

Acknowledge his or her brilliance.

Acknowledge his or her help in front of others.

Be willing to show your ignorance.

Focus on the Information-Keeper and not on yourself.

Check your attitude.

Be aware of his or her communication style.

CHAPTER SEVEN

PROCRASTINATING BEHAVIOR PROBLEMS

The motto of the Procrastinator is "Why do it now if I can put it off until tomorrow?" If the Procrastinator has promised to assist you on an important project, you're probably in trouble. The Procrastinator always seems to have an excuse, and seems genuinely to believe it. He is usually a victim of someone else's pressure, or so he thinks. The Procrastinator always has too much to do. He might say, "I would be a great success if I didn't have so much to slow me down." Many Procrastinators will make promises but never keep them.

The type of person who is most susceptible to a Procrastinator is someone who is very patient, who constantly believes the Procrastinator's excuses, and is willing to give him another chance.

The victim may be a bit indecisive himself, not knowing exactly what to do or say.

Here are a few basic strategies for dealing with Procrastinators:

1. Help the Procrastinator to clear up the piles of paper, so he or she can begin afresh.

2. If you work on projects together, ensure that he or she is using a diary system that works and is coordinated with yours.

3. Delegate projects with deadlines and get the Procrastinator to give you daily progress reports.

4. Talk about the fear of failure. The Procrastinator's philosophy might be: "If I don't do it, then I can't fail and I won't look like a fool."

5. Be supportive and not judgmental. Give positive feedback for even the smallest accomplishment.

6. Be specific in your requests and give real deadlines.

7. Make the Procrastinator responsible for the outcome if he does procrastinate: tell him that he will have to face the person who needs the work, or that he will have to stay late until it is completed.

8. Know that procrastination is a long-term habit and will not go away quickly. Always follow up to be sure the Procrastinator is not slipping behind.

In this chapter, we will discuss how to deal with three types of Procrastinator: Untruthfuls, Idlers, and Perfectionists.

• UNTRUTHFULS—HOW TO DEAL WITH PEOPLE WHO SAY THEY'LL DO IT BUT RARELY DO

Sometimes you don't know you are dealing with the Untruthful behavior problem until major damage has been done. The Untruthful seems to have a split personality. On the one hand he can be friendly, willing, and supportive, while on the other hand he has a negative attitude, and can withdraw his help. He may say, "Sure, I would love to spend Friday with you," but when Friday comes he will have made other plans and will act as if your previous agreement never existed. If there is an office party for someone, he may say, "Include me in on the present" but then when you go to collect the money he will deny it or say he just doesn't have the cash. By doing this, he leaves you out on a limb.

If you are a victim of the Untruthful, you may very well begin building a wall to protect yourself. Just when you get your wall in place he will begin doing what he promised. After he has followed through a few times, you let your wall down, and guess what? He will do it to you all over again.

Evelyn shared a story about a personal relationship that fell into this category. She had been dating Carl for two years. She was quite taken by him and did not want to believe that he was ever untruthful. She just kept believing what he said, always making excuses for his untruthfulness. Most of the incidents revolved around Carl saying he would do something—set business appointments, make calls, organize an event, pursue an idea—and then not following through. Evelyn found this very frustrating but kept hoping it would change. The final straw came when they planned a holiday together. Evelyn asked if he was sure he could pay his half, and after he had looked over his finances he said, "Absolutely." Well, when the bill came for the airfare, Carl said he could not pay his share. Evelyn, very upset, said, "But you told me you could afford to go." Carl's reply was: "I didn't tell a lie, I just said what I knew you wanted to hear!"

As is revealed in this story, many Untruthfuls are afraid of rejection, so they will say whatever it is they think you want to hear, regardless of the truth.

When dealing with an Untruthful, the most important thing to remember is: **Watch what they do, stop listening to what they say.** Once you watch their behavior and believe what you see instead of what you hear, you will be a much happier person.

Another variation of this behavior problem is the person with big plans. He is going to make a quick fortune, he guarantees this is a foolproof idea, he knows all the important people in the area and says you should certainly hook up with them. Be careful. Check the facts: you could be dealing with an Untruthful.

Sandy was definitely one of these people. She was always into some plan to get rich and include you in the set-up costs. Sandy had a great idea to help her friend Sharon get her new business going while, obviously, making lots of money herself. All of this would have been fine if it was actually going to happen—if Sandy would actually follow through. To cover herself, Sharon told Sandy that it was a good idea, but that if Sandy did not do anything to get it off the ground within sixty days, then she, Sharon, wanted to go ahead on her own. Sandy felt very angry and insulted that Sharon would imply that she would not follow through, and she refused to accept the deal. The bottom line was that Sandy did not follow through with her great plans, as usual, and Sharon went on her way and left her friend behind to waste someone else's time.

Try these basic strategies for dealing with Untruthfuls:

1. Establish whether someone's behavior is untruthful by being aware of how often this person does it. More than twice and you have a problem (twice is being generous; once is probably enough).

2. Watch what the Untruthful does, stop listening to what he or she says.

3. Ask a lot of questions starting with how, what, where, when, why, and how much. Try the following: "How do you know that?" "What makes you say that?" "Where did you get your information?" "When have you scheduled the appointment for?" "Why are you so sure about this?"

4. Let the Untruthful know you need the truth even if it is something he or she thinks you will not want to hear.

5. Make the person feel safe about telling you the truth.

6. Realize that the Untruthful has a strong need to be accepted.

7. Don't expect the behavior to change.

8. Don't accept nebulous answers.

SITUATION 1. My difficult person is someone who has a very different personality. One day she will work well, cooperate, and is very helpful. Another day she is angry, uncommunicative, morose, and will not work with others. To make it worse, on the bad days she lets others down by not following through on what she had committed to previously. *Rebecca.*

It is clear from the opening of this section that the personality Rebecca describes is not unique. This person is very sad and insecure, but with this type of behavior it is difficult to reach out and help. The behavior change seems to happen on the days when her previous commitments are due. She is offering her help in order to get acceptance and friends. However, when it comes down to it, she either can't or doesn't want to do the work.

Rebecca can start by reinforcing this person's behavior on her good days. She should not acknowledge the poor behavior on her bad days. It is important to avoid saying things like "What is wrong?" or "You seem upset, can I help?" This reinforces the attention she gets from her poor behavior. If there are commitments due on a bad day, Rebecca should ask for them in an assertive manner. She should not react to her negative behavior, but should let her know she is unhappy with the lack of follow-through. She should set boundaries to what she feels is acceptable. Also, on this person's good days, Rebecca could call a meeting to discuss what this mood change is about. Is it her fear of failure? Is it a personal issue, or possibly chemical? She should check all reasons for poor behavior before assuming that the person is just obnoxious. And, finally, Rebecca must remember to stay in the Freedom State at all times.

SITUATION 2. A colleague working in my previous position will backstab, tell lies, or do whatever she can to get what she wants but is "gushy" and very friendly to everyone—two-faced! How do you deal with that? *Rose.*

This colleague is untruthful with her actions but not with her words. Very "gushy" to make people like her, and more aggressive to get what she wants. The best thing for Rose to do is to leave it alone. She should not let the situation upset her because there is not much she can do to make her colleague change. Both of these opposing behaviors get her what she wants.

Rose is not alone in her opinion of her colleague. Other employees will back away when they work out that her behavior is not truthful and that she is doing whatever it takes to get her desired results. The most important thing for Rose to do is to take care of herself and avoid getting caught up in the situation.

SITUATION 3. David is a hard one to figure out. He says one thing convincingly and then does something else. My difficulty is that I cannot always see the game that he is playing. I usually see it later on when it is too late. *Harold.*

Harold should watch what David does, stop listening to what he says. This can be frightening because Harold keeps believing what David is saying, but circumstances have proved that he is an Untruthful. When David says something that Harold wants to believe, he should respond with, "That sounds great, David, but now what are you really going to do?" If David does not change his story, then Harold can proceed with the when, where, what, how, and why questions discussed at the beginning of this section. He should end with: "Let me know when you have finished." Harold should not raise his hopes, believing that this time David will do what he says.

Another approach is to get it in writing: "Great, David, but please write that down for me so there won't be any confusion." If Harold does not want to ask David to write it down, then he can make notes himself regarding the conversation and give David a copy with the traditional FYI (for your information) at the top.

Don't attack the Untruthful. Remember that he or she wants to be liked. Be confrontational in a very gentle way by asking questions, writing things down, etc., in an attempt to make the person responsible for his or her actions. Hopefully, this will help begin to break the habit.

Just one note of caution: You may get very good at watching what Untruthfuls do and not listening to what they say. Be careful not to treat others who are not Untruthfuls in the same way. This can get you into trouble. Become an expert listener and observer so that you are sure to communicate appropriately with each individual person in your life.

**Points to remember when dealing with
  Untruthfuls:**

Diagnose.

Watch what the Untruthful does, stop listening to
    what he or she says.

Ask questions.

Get things in writing.

Only accept clear answers.

Don't ignore the behavior.

Make the Untruthful feel safe about telling the truth.

Don't get hooked.

Remember, the Untruthful needs to be liked.

• IDLERS—HOW TO MAKE THEM GET ON WITH THE JOB AND STOP WASTING YOUR TIME

The Idler is very frustrating because his time-wasting usually affects your job. You need him to do something for you—complete a project, write a report, organize a meeting, or follow through on directions you have given him. Idlers can take forever to make a decision. Idlers avoid tasks that they feel are unimportant, regardless of your wishes. The Idler hopes that if he idles long enough, the project will disappear.

Another Idler may waste time because of bad habits, lack of rules to follow, or just plain disorganization. These Idlers may start one project, then stop in the middle, and move to another project without finishing either. Who picks up the pieces? Probably you, or else the projects will just fall through the cracks.

Your challenge is to get the Idler to change gear and move ahead. Try these basic strategies:

1. Get the Idler to tell you what he or she is thinking. Is the person nervous about failing? Is he angry? Does he not understand?

2. What is stopping this individual from making a decision or moving forward? Maybe he or she needs more information.

3. Ask questions about steps the Idler plans to follow: get details. This will help him take responsibility.

4. Make moving ahead easy by giving him information he may need. Ensure he has the whole picture.

5. Discuss the consequences of the Idler's time-wasting: "Jenny, not having the information on the Clark account is causing delays in billing. What do you suggest doing to solve this problem?"

6. When the Idler makes a decision, support her or him.

7. Watch for signs of frustration: fidgeting, silence, no eye contact.

8. As a last resort, outline consequences and stick to them.

A common problem is having a child who is an Idler. Almost everyone who has children has experienced this to some degree. This behavior can bring a mother or father to screaming demands. Does it work? Sometimes in the short term, but in the long term it causes anger, resentment, frustration, and a war of wills.

If your child is wasting time, ask yourself a few questions

before moving forward. How important is it that he does it the way I want? Will it matter this time next week or next year if he wastes more time than I feel he should? If it is not a major problem, then allow the child to be a child and achieve at his own speed. Compliment the completion of any job, regardless of how long it took, and don't add any "buts" to the end of your compliment: "Your book report looks great . . . but if you had not fooled around so much you would have had time to play." "Your room is so nice and clean . . . but you missed the film because it took you so long."

If the time-wasting seems extreme and will establish bad habits for adult life, then take appropriate steps to get this child moving. Ask questions. Discover if there is fear about doing something wrong. Maybe the child is just bored and needs to know how to get started. His or her time-wasting could be a way of getting attention. Children who want attention will take it in whatever form they can get it. Ensure that the child has enough of your time. Use a reward system for achievement (positive reinforcement). Do not punish (negative reinforcement).

SITUATION 4. Clients are slow in coming to a decision about a project or they make their start date too late. They then expect instant service, without any appreciation of the pressures on my organization to deliver. *Mike.*

There is a sign hanging in my printer's place of business that reads: "Your procrastination is not my rush." This seems appropriate for this type of client. In the case of my printer, he has more business than he wants or needs. If he loses a few customers because of this sign, it is not a problem for him. Mike should ask himself, "How important is this client to me?"

There are two business rules to consider:

1. The customer is always right.

2. If the customer is wrong, go back to Rule 1.

This is frustrating but true. Here are some steps that Mike can take:

1. Discuss with the client in advance how much time it will take to accomplish the project from the start date.

2. Get acknowledgment from the client of this time need: "It will take thirty days to complete this job. If you make your decision on the first of June, we will finish the project on the first of July. Do you understand?"

3. Ask the client what would make his decision easier.

4. Ensure that you are talking to the decision-making person.

5. Do as much for the client as you can, recalling the original business rules above.

6. Remember, the client's only concern is for his own interest. Don't take it personally.

SITUATION 5. I need help getting one of my staff to increase her output of work. She always seems to have too much to do, but I know she is not overworked. She wastes a lot of time, but it is difficult to bring this out into the open because she gives the impression of being so busy. *Christine.*

This person is a manipulative dealer. She fakes being busy to keep her workload to a minimum. Christine must be assertive when dealing with this staff member. Here are some steps to follow with this type of Idler:

1. Schedule a planning meeting with her.

2. Be very exact about needs and deadlines.

3. Give her a time log to fill out for a specific time period. This time log will help both Christine and her employee to see exactly how she spends her time. Below is an example. It can of course be changed to suit individual needs. It can be set out in fifteen-minute intervals for a difficult employee such as Christine's Idler. For other employees, it can be filled in two or three times a day and used as a way of evaluating their time individually.

4. Evaluate the time log together. Ask to see completed work.

TIME LOG			
DATE: MONDAY, JUNE 1			
TIME	WHAT I DID	VISITOR/ WHO/WHY	PHONE/ WHO/WHY
9:00–9:15	sorted mail		
9:15–9:30	typed for Sue		
9:30–9:45	typed for Sue	Mary needed file	
9:45–10:00	meeting with boss		Mr. Smith left message
10:00–10:15			
10:15–10:30			

5. Do not adopt a sympathetic approach. This will help eliminate the possibility of getting hooked by being seen as the "nice guy."

6. Keep communication very matter of fact and direct. Freedom State.

7. Be willing to approach this Idler even when she is acting very busy.

SITUATION 6. This person is a union representative. Sometimes he will work well, but most of the time his performance is unsatisfactory. He takes too long to complete assignments, does them incorrectly, says the job is finished but fails to put away the parts. His slow work wastes time, his mistakes waste time, and his incompletion wastes time. Can you help? *Paul.*

The best place to start with this Idler is at the beginning. Paul needs to take a hard look at the Idler's attitude. Everything mentioned in his difficult behavior problem points to a negative attitude: slow performance, mistakes, incompletion, and a general lack of caring and responsibility. The only hope of changing this Idler is by helping him improve his attitude. This might be a reflection of many issues, such as not enjoying his work, finding work too difficult, not being liked by others, or a general lack of self-confidence and self-esteem. The first step is to eliminate any problems of lack of information by clarifying what he is supposed to do, and how. When Paul is sure that all of this information is clear, then he can begin to help by developing a better working relationship. Below are some open-ended statements that can be used to increase openness, to clarify the feelings this person has about his job and to improve the work relationship. Paul might ask him to complete these statements openly and honestly. He could explain that this will help open a dialogue between the two of them. When the statements are completed, Paul and this member of staff can have a safe, nonjudgmental conversation.

1. Basically my job is . . .
2. Usually I am the kind of person who . . .
3. When things are going well . . .
4. I want to become the kind of person who . . .
5. In my job I'm best at . . .
6. My great weakness in my job is . . .
7. When I am supervising someone, I prefer . . .
8. Your job seems to be . . .
9. The best boss I ever had was . . .
10. The worst boss I ever had was . . .
11. I usually react to criticism by . . .
12. When I am approaching a deadline, I . . .
13. The person I am having the most trouble with is . . .
14. I need to . . .
15. I think you see me as . . .
16. If I could just . . .
17. My personal goals are . . .★★

It is helpful to have this type of dialogue every three to six months in order to achieve and maintain a better working relationship.

Points to remember when dealing with Idlers:

Find out what the Idler is thinking.

Find out what's stopping him or her.

Get specific details about his or her plans.

★★The numbered list is reprinted from J. W. Pfeiffer and J. E. Jones (eds.), *A Handbook of Structured Experiences for Human Relations Training,* Vol. IV (San Diego, Ca.: Pfeiffer & Company, 1973). Used with permission.

Make things easy for him or her.

Support the Idler.

Set deadlines in advance.

Get the Idler to acknowledge deadlines.

Use a time log.

Be assertive.

Set consequences.

Ask questions to develop a better working
relationship.

• PERFECTIONISTS—HOW TO DEAL WITH "IT MUST BE PERFECT SO IT NEVER GETS DONE" BEHAVIOR

The procrastinating Perfectionist is a person who rarely completes a project on time because it is just not up to his high standards. He will do it over and over again to be sure it is perfect, but perfection, in his eyes, is virtually impossible to reach! Sometimes he will not start on a project because he knows that this perfect process is too difficult. He worries about every little aspect of the assignment. The request "Give me an overview" is enough to send him into orbit because an overview can never be perfect. The Perfectionist tends to be a Technocrat (see Chapter 1). He focuses on the details and loses sight of the bigger picture. He would like everyone to leave him alone and stop harrassing him, so that he can work at his own speed. A Perfectionist would not think of taking on a new job unless he knew every aspect of the work required before he started.

Sometimes a Perfectionist only shows this behavior in one area, such as work assignments. But many behave this way in every aspect of their lives. Their desks are perfect, their appointment calendars exact, their closets as neat as a pin. All of this organization may look great but it can cause major delays and a lot of anxiety, and it involves very little risk taking.

Ron was a Perfectionist. Nothing was good enough. Whatever assignment he was given, he would look into it so deeply that in the time it took him to work through the first stage, his partner could have completed that assignment as well as three more! The partnership had developed because Ron was the thinking person and his partner, Merl, was the doing person. The problems occurred when Merl wanted Ron to be a doer too. Doers tend to intimidate thinkers (Perfectionists) and can make them more insecure about their thinking by pushing all the time. This slows them down even more and lowers their self-esteem. The relationship did not last. Merl became so frustrated with Ron's perfectionism that he decided to find a new partner. In retrospect, Merl says he wishes he had been able to accept the differences because Ron was very good at thinking through details, a quality which is difficult to find.

This story demonstrates the frustrations that a Perfectionist and his associates can feel. Patience is important when dealing with a Perfectionist, but there is a limit. Here are some strategies for dealing with Perfectionists.

1. Get the Perfectionist to keep a time log (he or she will do it perfectly).

2. Set time requirements in advance.

3. Let the person know that his or her idea of perfect may be too expensive for the organization (time = money).

4. Inform him that opportunities do not last forever, and he must move fast.

5. Tell her that perfection is not always a company standard: for many, task completion within a given time is what's important.

6. Break the projects down into small sections and request each completed section individually. This will help you to see how much the Perfectionist has achieved and will make him or her feel good with each completion.

SITUATION 7. A high-level manager in the organization is critical of others, ultracautious, avoids vulnerable situations. She makes no contributions unless she is 100 percent certain of the facts. She can't generalize or accept generalizations. She will only deal in absolutes. *Gregory.*

The fact that this is a high-level manager does present a problem and makes things more difficult. Gregory should work at communicating in a way that she understands: direct, factual using no generalizations. This person is another Technocrat and does not want to hear concepts or ideas unless they can be substantiated by fact. I'd advise Gregory to put ideas on paper, structuring them with a beginning, a middle, and an ending, and letting the manager know exactly what Gregory plans to achieve. It's a good idea to ask her for feedback, to let her know that her decisions are respected (Gregory might cite a specific decision he can honestly say he agreed with). He should be silent when this manager is critical of others, as he may find himself on the receiving end of criticism. This woman has achieved her position by being careful and Gregory will not change this. He should take whatever steps he can to build the relationship, and stop wishing that this person was different.

SITUATION 8. This subordinate is very intelligent and proud. He spends too much time on large projects, making sure they are perfect. He carefully avoids more mundane duties. I don't think his avoiding is deliberate, because he is so engrossed in these other projects, but I am feeling resentful because I usually end up doing all the work he does not do because of the time his perfectionism takes. *Maggie*.

Maggie's subordinate is smart and manipulative. Her biggest problem is that she does the work he does not complete. She must stop this. She can use the model in chapter 4.

1. Tell him he is not doing the less exciting duties required for his job and describe them specifically.

2. Let him know that not doing these duties is ineffective because someone else, usually Maggie, must leave her own work to complete his work.

3. Tell him exactly what she needs is for all his work to be done by . . . and give a deadline.

4. Ask how he will do this.

5. Get a commitment from him to change his present procrastinating behavior.

6. Repeat this commitment back to him.

7. Set a time to reevaluate his performance.

8. End by telling him what a good job he does on his big projects. Leave him feeling really good that he has agreed to complete all his work and how pleased she is to have this man in her department.

The resentful feelings Maggie has toward him are actually toward herself, caused by the fact that she is not standing up to him. She should examine what is stopping her, be willing to step into her discomfort zone (the zone we most want to avoid) and tell him what she expects.

SITUATION 9. Demands are made on me that need my complete attention. I am under pressure to do many tasks all at the same time. I want to do a good job and need to do projects one at a time. How can I convince my boss to leave me alone? *Katherine.*

This difficult situation looks at the issue from a Perfectionist point of view. It helps us to see how Katherine feels—frustrated, overworked and not listened to.

Katherine needs to ask herself, "How good is good?" If her boss is giving her more work, it could be a sign that she is doing a very good job to begin with. It is great that she wants to do the best job possible. To help her stay sane, Katherine should:

1. Talk to her boss and tell him her feelings and needs.

2. Keep a time log for a week to show him how her time is spent.

3. Keep track of interruptions to see if some time can be saved: for example, waiting in her boss's office while he is on the phone, social interruptions, answering someone else's phone.

4. Suggest viable ways to lighten her workload.

5. Ensure that she is willing to do a job well enough rather than perfectly all the time.

6. Delegate where possible. She shouldn't ask, "Who can do this job the best?" because that will be her, of course. Instead she might ask, "Who can do this job well enough?" and then give it to that person.

Points to remember when dealing with Perfectionists:

Work closely with a Perfectionist to help move him or her along.

Get the person to keep a time log.

State time requirements immediately.

Time = money: let her know.

Remind him that the company standard is
completeness.

Break large projects into small.

Communicate factually.

Don't do the Perfectionist's incomplete work for him
or her.

Stop wishing the person was different.

CHAPTER EIGHT

NEGATIVE-COMPLAINING BEHAVIOR PROBLEMS

There are many different types of Negative characters: quiet Guilt-Givers, moody Whiners, outspoken Idea-Destroyers. It is inevitable that at some time in your life you will have to deal with someone who approaches most situations with a negative point of view. These people can ruin the brightest of days, the best ideas, and the most adventurous soul. The Negative person goes through life disappointed in advance. He has rationalized the fact that because there are no guarantees in life, he must always be prepared for the worst. He has discovered that no one will save him from problems, no one can be counted on 100 percent, and that therefore the opposite is true: nothing will ever go smoothly, nothing will go as he has planned. This is his way of protecting himself. Some typical statements from a Negative person are: "That's a ridiculous idea." "How could you even consider going there?" "I can't do that, it's impossible." The Negative person does not come up with a productive alternative to his idea-destroying. He just can't accept matters as they are or see a way out.

You may find yourself trapped by a Negative person because your first instinct was to find a solution to each of their negative statements. For example, if a Negative person says, "I can't do that, it's impossible," a response that might trap you is: "Of course you can, I'll call . . . ," or "It's easy if we just . . . ," or, perhaps, "I am sure it is possible if you just do . . ." All these responses try to remedy the Negative person's reasons for being miserable. Do not get hooked, do not attempt to fix the problem. Instead, respond by saying: "Okay, I'll give it to Mary, she wanted to do it . . . ," or "That's too bad, we're making these changes on Friday."

Other ways to avoid the traps of a Negative person are:

1. Ignore the negative statements as if they have not been said.

2. Don't let the Negative person's concerns direct your actions.

3. Don't catch his or her negative attitude.

These are the strategies for dealing with Negative people:

1. Get the Negative person to tell you his worst-case scenario (it will normally never happen).

2. Surround the Negative person with positive people who will not try to remedy his or her negativism.

3. Identify why he or she is negative: is it because of long-term problems, personal problems, dislike for another employee?

4. Get him help: try self-esteem training, personal counseling.

5. Make the person responsible for decisions and outcomes.

In this chapter we will discuss how to deal with Whiners, Idea-Destroyers, and Guilt-Givers.

• WHINERS—HOW TO AVOID GETTING TRAPPED BY WHINING PEOPLE

Whining people are like fingernails on the blackboard, grating on your nerves. You may want to make them happy but it does not seem possible no matter how hard you try. They hate any type of change—weather, traffic, job, relationship, home—because if they look far enough ahead they can always see disaster. Their answering-machine voice can sound so depressing you hate to leave a message. The whiners have a lot of "if onlys." If only I had got married, if only I had moved (or hadn't moved), if only I had a better job, if only I had more money, if only . . . if only . . . if only. . . . If only, you are thinking, you would just change your attitude!

The problem with whining people is that they do seem to have many negative things happen to them. Is it the attitude that brings on the bad experiences or the bad experiences that bring on the negative attitude? Think about this for a minute. Do you know people who have had a hard time but keep on moving ahead in a relatively happy state? I hope so. All of us have negative things happen in our lives. Every bad experience should not be seen as a reason for therapy, but be seen as a normal part of life. The truly successful person is the one who deals with the situation and moves on. This person does not wallow in the mud of depression. We are all allowed a period of negativism or whining, but the problem comes when it is constant, when the positive attitude is rarely seen.

Eve was a real pain in the neck. She whined about everything. "I hate my job, they are terrible to me" (and they were). New job, same story. Next job, same story again. She would ask, "How can Celia get all the attention? She isn't even attractive. Why don't these men ask me out?" Her facial expression was always tight, with a deep wrinkle between her eyes. Nothing was fun or worth the effort. Vacations were rare, and usually ended with: "This wasn't a good choice, I wish I hadn't gone?" Not many friends found it easy to be with Eve because it was such a downer. But there was one person who stuck by her, Mary. Mary found a redeeming quality in Eve's whining and negative attitude. This quality was Eve's ability to take criticism and not run away. She would listen to what Mary had to say about her whining and began to see what she was doing to herself and her life. A typical conversation between the two might go like this:

> Eve: "Nothing will change, my life is miserable, why can't I meet a man?"
> Mary: "How could you expect to meet a man when you are so miserable? Stop whining and do something about it."
> Eve: "I can't do anything to change things. I am miserable, just miserable."
> Mary: "You must love being miserable, because you just carry on in the same way all the time."

At this point most Whiners would tell Mary to get lost and then go and look for someone else to support them in their misery. But not Eve.

> Eve: "I don't love it. Why do you say that?"
> Mary: "You tell me when you haven't felt like a victim of your own life."

Eve: "Well I can see your point, but it hurts. What is a person supposed to do? I have never known anything different."
Mary: "Let's look at what you want to do."

This friendship has survived for more than ten years. During this time Eve has pursued different forms of personal help to break her habit of looking at the world through dark glasses.

When Eve begins whining again, Mary tells her she does not want to spend time with her if she is going to be miserable. She will listen to constructive conversation but not destructive whining. This friendship has endured through many ups and downs, but neither Eve nor Mary runs away. Their story is just one example of dealing with a long-term Whiner. There is an investment, but it is worth it.

There are some basic strategies for dealing with Whiners:

1. Don't fall for their whining. Try: "I have heard that before, what are you going to do about it?"

2. Let the Whiner know that he or she cannot bring you a problem without a potential solution.

3. Discover what the "real problem" is. Be careful: Do not encourage more whining.

4. Make the Whiner responsible. Don't fix things for this person.

5. Get the Whiner to write a list of all his or her worries, and next to each worry, how he or she will deal with it.

6. Don't imagine this behavior will change on its own.

SITUATION 1. A colleague, John, is never satisfied with any job. He looks at the negative side of everything, complaining to anyone and everyone. He brings up grievances all the time. *Sue.*

This worker could be a strong negative influence in the office if he is not dealt with appropriately. The first strategy for dealing with any difficult person is honest confrontation. Sue should talk to John about his attitude. She mustn't get into a "solving all his issues" conference, but should see if she can get a clue to his general miserable attitude. If this doesn't give her a clue or it seems hopeless, she should move on to Plan 2: ignore him, and tell others to ignore him also. John should be made aware that Sue will not listen to him unless he has a positive statement to make. If he begins complaining, she should walk away as if he were not there. This is a long-term habit: John has learned to get attention by being negative. Sue should reinforce any positive behavior she sees. If John has a real grievance, she might ask him to write it down and suggest three possible solutions. Sue must be firm and not waver into sympathy for all his complaints.

SITUATION 2. An employee has a very negative attitude at work. He constantly complains instead of offering potential solutions. He appears always to be in a bad mood, is difficult to approach, and has the effect of lowering general morale. *Clarence.*

Ahhhhhh, another delightful person. Let's deal with the difficulty Clarence has in approaching him. One of the reasons that the negative whining person uses this behavior is to keep others away. If he is always in a bad mood, then maybe no one will give him any more work or responsibility. He can build a cocoon around himself. It must work, or else he would not continue to behave in this way. The first step is for Clarence to cut right through John's behavior with his needs and requests. It is an uncomfortable thing to do, but it is necessary. Here is how it might work:

Clarence: "Here is the project information. I need your work completed by tomorrow."

Employee (appearing angry and hostile): "Good luck. I have too much to do now, and, besides, this is a ridiculous project."

Clarence: "Three-thirty tomorrow will be fine."

Employee: "This will never work. These projects are a waste of time."

Clarence (acknowledge and move on): "I understand you are not happy. I expect it tomorrow at three-thirty." (Now leave the office.) Review Chapter 4.

If he is negative in a meeting, Clarence should state publicly, "I hear your disagreement. If you have a positive solution, great, otherwise please do not disrupt the meeting."

None of these solutions I have discussed is easy. Any type of behavior adjustment takes an incredible amount of concentration and effort. What you are being asked to do is to change your behavior toward the difficult person. Remember that when you change, he will have to change too.

SITUATION 3. Joe is a colleague, a very generous person who would do anything for you. During the workday he keeps coming to me with problems or something that has to be attended to. He seems to me to have to solve a problem each day. He always interrupts what you are doing at the time. He is still a nice person. *Neville.*

There *are* some nice whiners, and here is a good example. Difficult behavior does not have to be obnoxious in order to be stressful. Joe is a person who wants attention. He wants acknowledgment for his presence and for the job that he is doing. Next time Joe brings Neville a problem, Neville should stop what he is doing and talk for a few minutes about how the two of them can change this situation. For instance, Neville could:

1. Choose a specific time each day when Joe can come to him with his problems. Making him wait for this time will help him to come up with the answer himself.

2. Let Joe know that he doesn't mind helping, but that he knows how intelligent Joe is and that he can probably solve some of these problems without Neville's help.

3. Ask Joe to make a note on what he is accomplishing and leave it for him. This way he will get acknowledgment for his effort without involving Neville in his work process.

Remember, people are *motivated by* acknowledgment and approval more than they are motivated by money.

Points to remember when dealing with Whiners:

Don't fall for the whining.

Ask for a solution.

Discuss the Whiners's real issue.

Don't fix things for him or her.

Reinforce positive behavior.

Be firm.

Step through the Whiner's negative barrier.

Be consistent.

• IDEA-DESTROYERS—HOW TO EXPRESS YOUR IDEAS AND PLANS SUCCESSFULLY WHEN IN THE PRESENCE OF A DESTROYER

Idea-Destroyers choose this method of control for several different reasons. Most often idea-destroying is used as a shield for the Idea-Destroyer's own incompetence. If they can keep you from accomplishing your ideas, they will not feel so bad about their own lack of inspiration. Idea-Destroyers are very open-minded if you agree with them; otherwise, watch out! Idea-Destroyers tend to operate independently, or with other Idea-Destroyers, and refuse to take orders. They may hide behind procedures in order to avoid certain responsibilities or to stop you dead in your tracks: "Dave, you must have read the procedures for Project A. It is clear that you are working in Don's area. I don't know how you think you can do that even if you are bored." An Idea-Destroyer only works within the exact structure of the rules. He does not understand the concept of working within the spirit of the rules.

Another type of Idea-Destroyer is the person who has real difficulty with anyone else getting credit for achievement. He is competent and has good ideas, but he wants to be seen by management as the only results-oriented employee. He could be the type of person who, while at school, was an achiever but had few friends. He will do whatever it takes to be number one, even if it means hurting people or ruining their plans. This type of Idea-Destroyer has self-confidence in the work area but has trouble with communication and emotional issues. He is a tyrant as a manager but can be liked by superiors for his achievements. His personal life is likely to be a disaster.

Try these basic strategies when dealing with Idea-Destroyers:

1. Use the "broken-record" response to an idea-destroying statement: "I understand how you

feel, but I believe this is an idea worth pursuing," "Yes, I understand what you are saying but I will be going ahead with this idea," "Uh huh, I can see your point of view, but I feel strongly about this"; then close with "Was there anything else you wanted to clarify?" Don't let the Idea-Destroyer wear you down. Just keep repeating your broken-record reply.

2. Be aware of the idea-destroying game and realize that you need to change your tactics with this person.

3. Don't share your idea with the Idea-Destroyer, if at all possible.

4. Get support from others prior to the presentation of your idea. There is strength in numbers.

5. Counter negative statements with a preplanned statement: "Don, I'd like you to wait until the end of the meeting to give your opinion." Then, if he tries again, go to the broken-record behavior and keep repeating this statement.

6. Face him directly about his idea-destroying tactics: "Don, I am aware of the lack of your support for any of my ideas. I wonder if it is something I am doing that is causing this?" Keep the conversation in the "I am feeling" mode, rather than the "You did it to me" mode.

7. Be assertive; your ideas are worth hearing.

SITUATION 4. My difficult person is a colleague who is always criticizing my ideas or asking critical questions along the lines of "Why did you do it that way?" I tend to stay calm, although I feel very defensive. I answer his questions but often feel like turning the situation around to put him on the defensive, even though that is not my style. *Eileen.*

It is easy to understand why Eileen would like to turn this situation around. Feeling attacked or put down is frustrating. In order to resolve things without losing her calm demeanor or changing her style, Eileen must stop answering all his questions. She is giving him the control he wants by letting him put her on the defensive. Here are some alternative responses she could try:

1. Do not answer his question; just look at him in silence. This may be enough to get the message across. After a moment of silence, continue as if the question has not been asked.

2. If he asks, "Why are you looking at me that way?" then respond with, "I am wondering why you asked me that question." Focus on his need to ask unnecessary questions, not on the questions themselves.

3. If he criticizes, prepare a broken-record statement as discussed earlier in this section, and be ready with it.

Eileen should expect to feel stressed when she begins to respond differently. In time, she will get comfortable with her newfound power in this situation.

SITUATION 5. X always starts off any discussion or meeting with reasons why the proposal under discussion is ill-advised, unworkable, and not in the best interests of the organization (unless it is a proposal that he has come up with himself). *Ted.*

X sounds like the second type of Idea-Destroyer discussed at the beginning of this section. Nothing is good enough unless it is his idea. Preparation is the only chance Ted has to get his proposal accepted. He should get support from other colleagues before any meeting. If the meeting is only with X, Ted should have documentation to prove why his idea would be in the best interests of the organization: how it would save money, time, etc. He should be as specific as possible. If there is a way to include X as part of the proposal, to make him look good too, Ted should do it. But he should keep his own name on any written material regarding the proposal.

X could have a difficult time with change. He may feel out of control unless it is his change that is being considered. In this case, Ted needs to get these issues out in the open at the beginning: "I know new ideas make you feel uncomfortable, and I understand your point of view, but I think you will appreciate that this plan will make a major difference."

SITUATION 6. The problem I have is older team members who are constantly negative about new ideas. This attitude can and does affect younger team members. *Doug.*

This situation seems to reflect the concept of "You can't teach an old dog new tricks." Don't believe it! The belief that "We have always done it this way and we don't want to change" is a difficult one to alter, but with time and patience it can be done. Here are some ways for Doug to approach the "change" issue:

1. Have new ideas presented at an "ideas" meeting, not at other general meetings. This way Doug will have control by knowing that the negativity expressed by older team members will be entirely focused on this meeting.

2. Ask each old team member to think of one of the changes he has observed in past years that has had a positive effect on his job. Tell them that the reason

for doing this is to motivate the newer team members.

3. Begin the meeting by discussing the success of change over the past years. Doug, as leader of the meeting, should have one or two success stories prepared.

4. Now is Doug's chance to link their success stories with the changes of the present and future.

5. Open the meeting to new ideas.

6. If negativity continues, set a rule that no negative statement is to be made without a positive workable solution.

7. Partner each old team member with a new team member in any "ideas" session.

Change is something that most people fight, but it will happen, whether they do anything or not. Doug should help the "old guard" to see how change is inevitable, and can be positive. He should be prepared to follow this procedure more than once. If he perseveres, and is patient, this situation will change too.

Points to remember when dealing with Idea-Destroyers:

Use the "broken-record" response.

Change your tactics.

Get support for your ideas.

Ignore the destroying statement.

Focus on the need to destroy.

Be assertive.

Stop answering attacking questions.

Help the Idea-Destroyer to get comfortable with change.

Be prepared.

• GUILT-GIVERS—LEARN HOW TO REJECT THE GIFT OF GUILT

Guilt-Givers have learned how to avoid responsibility for any of their mistakes by pointing the finger at you. They will keep pointing the finger at you, and include anyone else who will accept the gift of guilt, in order to save their reputations. The Guilt-Giver will dig himself a very deep hole by pushing guilt on to you, but it does stop him from doing something he hates even more: apologizing! The following story is typical of a Guilt-Giver.

Janette and her family attended the wedding of Janette's cousin, Eileen. It was a lovely affair, with dinner and all the trimmings. Janette and her family were invited to sit in the family section and proudly did so. But as the months went by, Eileen received no wedding gift or card from Janette. Six months later, at another family event, Janette took Eileen aside, and said, "I have never received a thank-you card for my gift, and I just wondered what had happened." Eileen responded: "I never received your gift: my thank yous went out immediately." Janette stated that she had sent a gift certificate, and promised to send another one immediately. Eileen has still never received anything from Janette. Janette's family is unaware of her neglect and guilt-giving tactics. Eileen feels angry that Janette would try to place the blame on her rather than being honest and saying, "Oh, I feel so terrible, money was tight and time slipped by. Will you please accept my apology for not acknowledging your marriage? I want to make it up to you by . . ."

Guilt-Givers often cover their mistakes in this way. It is not a one-time situation but an ongoing habit of evading responsibility. Why did Eileen let this go by? How could she have passed the guilt back to Janette? The first issue is that of family, and not wanting to cause permanent offense. But whether it is family or work, offense is caused either way. If you do not say anything to the Guilt-Givers, you stay angry and barriers go up. If you do say something, the Guilt-Giver is likely to become indignant and will put up his own barriers to save his reputation. It seems to be an "I lose and you lose" situation. How can you turn it around into an "I win and you win" scenario?

There is an answer but it is not easy. In this situation, Eileen acted appropriately at the time by stating that she had not received the gift. This gave Janette every opportunity to redeem herself. However, when a further month had gone by with no gift, Eileen should have dropped a note to Janette stating that she had not received the gift as of today, and did not want Janette to think she wasn't grateful for something she had never received. This would keep things out in the open, and would certainly make Eileen feel good. It would also allow Janette to save face by realizing she must either be honest or correct the situation. The end result would be "I win and you win" (*not* "I'm happy and you're happy"): Eileen wins because she did not accept the situation and spoke up, and Janette wins because she will not have to lie any more—she will either own up, or send an acknowledgment.

Here are a few basic strategies for dealing with Guilt-Givers:

1. Give back the guilt. Politely, and without attacking the Guilt-Giver, state the truth.

2. Don't give in once you have given back the guilt. The Guilt-Giver may try another tactic. Repeat your truth again.

3. Separate yourself from the Guilt-Giver. Stay out of the line of fire.

4. Provide a gracious way out for your Guilt-Giver. Allow the person to save his or her reputation.

5. If you did deserve a portion of the guilt, accept it.

6. Keep a close watch on the Guilt-Giver's progress during work: you will then be able to stop any guilt-giving which has occurred because of procrastination and a need to cover up.

SITUATION 7. My boss tends to be emotional and unprofessional if she is in the wrong. She goes on the attack and makes me feel guilty for her mistakes. This seems to make the situation worse. *Helen.*

Dealing with a Guilt-Giving boss takes some special tactics. Helen does not want to jeopardize her position, but she does want to protect her own reputation. She should start by saying how she feels and letting her boss know that she is upset by her statements.

Helen can protect her boss by giving her an escape hatch, a way to save face. She is feeling inadequate, and the only way she knows to deal with these feelings is to put her mistakes on to others. If this style of guilt-giving has worked in the past she will continue to use it until it is more comfortable to do something new.

Helen must not just let it pass. She should ask for a few minutes of her boss's time to discuss the situation. A diplomatic approach might be: "I am feeling upset at the comments you made about my inadequacy on Project A. You have always agreed that my work is better than adequate and I have always considered you fair. Would you like to discuss the specific areas where we can make some changes? It's very important to me that we don't have any misunderstandings in our communication." This shows that

Helen cares about the relationship and wants to help the situation. It also shows that she will not sit back and accept the guilt for her boss's mistakes.

SITUATION 8. This person always uses the most innocent remarks to stir up trouble. He makes me feel guilty and very defensive and I find it very difficult to communicate. His mood swings make it impossible to anticipate reactions. *Valerie.*

Guilt-giving can be done in an innocent style as well as a more aggressive way. It is still guilt-giving and it tends to make you angry unless you respond. The innocent style is less overt and probably more difficult to respond to because the person seems so nice. You may even think he does not realize what he is doing. No such luck. He knows *exactly* what he is doing.

Let us focus on Valerie's situation. At the first statement, she should stop the Guilt-Giver by asking him, "What did you mean by that?" or "I'd like you to explain that to me." If she lets him go on for a few minutes before realizing that she has missed a guilt-giving statement, she should stop him then refer back to the beginning: "What was that you said a minute ago about . . . ? Please explain what you meant." If he responds with, "Oh, I didn't really mean that," then Valerie can reply, "Oh good, I just wanted to be sure."

Valerie should remember that she will have to do this many times before the Guilt-Giver realizes that she will not be a victim of his innocent behavior. She shouldn't worry whether his mood is good or bad, but should just stick to her tactics for dealing with this situation, and everything will begin to change.

SITUATION 9. My difficult person is an employee who insists that he is being picked on by his superiors. He is constantly attempting to lay guilt on them for his own shortcomings. He has had four or five supervisors whom he imagines are against him. *Frank.*

This situation is clear because of its history. When an employee is having trouble with one boss, it is sometimes difficult to know where the problem really lies. But when it happens again and again, it is pretty easy to diagnose: the employee is obviously the problem. To remedy the situation, Frank might:

1. Plan a face-to-face meeting with the employee.

2. Prepare by having documentation of this employee's work problems. He should not use this documentation unless it is the only way to bring the employee out of denial.

3. State what he has observed and do not let the employee point the finger at his supervisors.

4. Be sympathetic.

5. Find out if the work is too difficult for the employee, if he needs more information to do the job required, or if there are personal issues that keep him from doing the work.

6. Get an acknowledgment from him about his shortcomings. Frank must make it safe for the employee to do this. No judgments, only solutions.

7. Discuss how these shortcomings can be remedied.

8. Make a written contract between himself and the employee outlining what the latter will do and when.

9. Schedule regular follow-up meetings. Show continued support.

10. Validate the employee's achievements. Do not focus on the negatives. This employee is likely to

have low self-esteem, and if Frank can help him without judging him he will begin to improve.

Points to remember when dealing with Guilt-Givers:

Give the guilt back.

Don't let a guilt statement go by.

Separate yourself from the Guilt-Giver.

Accept responsibility if you are guilty.

Allow the Guilt-Giver a way out.

Ask questions.

Confront the Guilt-Giver.

Be consistent.

CHAPTER NINE

ARROGANT BEHAVIOR PROBLEMS

You have, no doubt, come across someone who is a Credit-Stealer, a Know-All, or a Show-Off, all behaviors common for the Arrogant person. Whatever idea you have, they come up with a better one. Or how about the person who has always had a more dangerous, more exciting, more extravagant, or more serious experience than you? No matter how creative you are in your storytelling, the Arrogant person is unimpressed and does whatever he can to bring the attention back to himself.

There are two major reasons why someone is arrogant:

1. A person who has gained great success very quickly.
   Whether the success is due to hard work,

intelligence, or good luck, this person feels he has all the answers. Many people who become successful are not arrogant, but it is easy to recognize those who have let success go to their heads.

2. A lack of self-esteem. This type of person never feels good enough inside, so must do everything he or she can to look good on the outside. This individual needs attention, but instead of getting the attention he wants, his arrogance causes other people to shun him.

Alexandra is arrogant. She always has an answer for whatever issue you bring up. She knows everything, and is sure that the next idea will make a million. She does all she can to get you involved: not because she is generous, but because she knows she cannot do it alone, though she will never admit it.

After spending quite a bit of time with Alexandra it became clear that her behavior reflects both of the above reasons for being arrogant. She started her own business and initially made a lot of money. However, she needed to impress others, so she rented a large office, hired help, leased a new car, moved into a big home, and bought a wardrobe of new clothes. She did not pay much attention to her mounting bills and before she knew it she was so much in debt that she could not recover and had to close her business. Every time she starts up again, she falls into the same trap: arrogance, overspending, and failure.

Alexandra's mother has always saved her financially while telling her she is useless. This has been the core reason for Alexandra's lack of self-esteem. She feels she needs to prove to everyone that she can succeed, that she is someone.

Getting to know Alexandra was a four-stage process: 1) being initially impressed by her apparent intelligence and her appearance of success; 2) beginning to experience the arrogant attitude and realizing that all that glitters is not gold; 3) wondering how to break loose; 4) understanding that her problems compelled her to behave this way.

Once you understand why Alexandra or someone like her is arrogant, you then have options. Some people may choose to stay involved with this person and take the opportunity to develop their own communication skills. Others may decide to break off their association in order to keep their sanity.

Arrogant personalities can't see what they are doing. If you try to tell them, they will not hear what you say. They are too wrapped up in themselves. If you want to get the credit you deserve and keep your self-esteem, read on. Be willing to do what it takes to avoid being the victim of the Credit-Stealer, the Know-All, and the Show-Off, all arrogant behavior types.

• CREDIT-STEALERS—HOW TO RECEIVE THE CREDIT YOU DESERVE WHILE IN THE PRESENCE OF A CREDIT-STEALER

Credit-Stealers will take credit for any work they do, as well as the credit for your work. You may not be aware that there is a competition going on, but the Credit-Stealer is definitely out to win. He feels rejection when your ideas are accepted instead of his. This rejection encourages him to pursue credit wherever he can. He probably feels he actually deserves credit, and if you bring his credit-stealing to his attention, he may consider for a moment shining a little light on you. But don't count on it. He will probably say that he doesn't know what you mean and may well get angry at your insinuations. Credit-Stealers are masters at looking good for upper management because they know when to speak up and blow their own horn.

Try these basic strategies when dealing with Credit-Stealers:

1. Be assertive. Speak up when a Credit-Stealer is taking credit for your work.

2. Document your accomplishments and ideas. If you are sharing an idea with a group, have it typed out, with your name on it of course, and give a copy to each person. This will make you look organized and prepared while warding off the Credit-Stealer.

3. Be professional. Don't develop an arrogant attitude toward your Credit-Stealer.

4. Give credit to others publicly, including the known Credit-Stealer.

5. Have a face-to-face meeting with your Credit-Stealer. Let him or her know how you feel but do not attack the person. "Fred, I am very upset. I can't understand what I have done to make you feel you needed to take credit for my project. Can you explain?"

6. Don't believe that the Credit-Stealer will disappear.

SITUATION 1. My three staff members do not get along. They constantly try to put one over on one another. They are more focused on individual credit than team accomplishments. Being a young manager, I find it hard to distance myself and handle this difficult situation. *Veronica.*

These three employees have developed the need to protect themselves from one another, rather than working together as a team. This may have started before Veronica arrived. Some managers believe that conflict inspires greatness, with each person trying to be better than the other. But as Veronica has experienced, this does not work in the long run.

What can Veronica do to change these poorly functioning individuals into a productive team?

1. Plan a meeting with the three staff members.

2. Give them one large project to work on together.

3. Get them to work together for one hour a day to plan what individual steps each should take to accomplish the goal.

4. Tell them that they will be evaluated as a team, and that no individual recognition will be given. Whatever positive or negative results are achieved will fall equally on each person's shoulders and records.

5. Do not listen to any complaints without all three present.

6. Schedule review meetings with the three and get positive feedback regarding their project.

7. In the review meetings, ask staff member A to report what staff member B has done; next ask staff member B what staff member C has done; and last ask staff member C what staff member A has done. This may sound childish, but it will make each person responsible for being involved in what his two colleagues are doing.

Even though Veronica is a young manager, this problem can be solved. With each experience, the skills for handling this and other difficult situations will become more polished. Veronica should keep practicing the Freedom State and should always show sensitivity to the needs of employees.

SITUATION 2. It is difficult to combat a coworker who does little work. He caters to the manager so well that he is considered the fair-haired boy. Others do not get the recognition they deserve. *Tom.*

The solution to this difficult situation will be focused in two different directions, based on the extent of Tom's involvement.

1. If Tom is not directly involved in this situation, if he is not losing credit himself, and if he is not managing anyone who is being affected by this worker, he should leave it alone. This person will fall on his face eventually. Tom should get on with his own work and let others who are directly affected handle the situation themselves.

2. If this worker is directly affecting Tom, action should be taken. Tom should examine what style of communication he is using and compare it with that of the fair-haired boy. Is Tom quiet and reserved? Does he feel that management should recognize his talents without him having to tell them? It is obvious from the amount of attention he gets that his coworker is outgoing and talkative. He is probably a Cellular Phone Communicator described in Chapter 1.

Tom needs to be seen and heard more. First, he should document any important projects he is working on, and give a copy to the manager with an FYI note attached. This will increase Tom's opportunities for more input. He should practice getting at least one point across in meetings. He should not stay quiet because he knows that someone else will cover his topic. He must be heard, otherwise he is invisible. When the coworker steals credit for Tom's work, he must speak up in a very polite manner. An ideal response in this type of situation is: "Excuse me, Fred, you're talking about the information I gave you. I am glad you brought it up, because I had that down on my agenda for today." Or, "Oh, Fred, I am so glad you agree with the information I gave you, I was hoping to discuss that today."

This is not easy, and takes preparation and practice. But it is the only way to change the situation.

SITUATION 3. I am very frustrated at meetings. Every time I bring up an idea, one specific colleague always jumps in and takes over. It ends up sounding like his idea. I feel very angry but do not know what to do. He keeps getting the pay raises I deserve! *Katherine.*

It sounds as if Katherine is dealing with a Bulldozer, someone who rolls over people to get what he wants! The most important thing here is to stop this colleague from interrupting. Again, this will take perserverance and practice, because he will not give in easily. Here are a few ideas to help Katherine stop the credit-stealing:

1. Decide how important this is to you. Do you want to get the pay raises you deserve? Do you want to be seen as the idea person? Be very clear about your worth. Once you perceive yourself as completely worthy of the recognition, then you will have the personal strength to change this situation.

2. Stop the interruptions. How, you ask? By interrupting back. When the colleague jumps in and takes over, stop him in his tracks. Don't wait for a pause in the conversation—for example: "John, John, you interrupted me, please let me finish explaining my idea." John will probably jump in a second time. Stop him again. "John, you

are interrupting me again. Please let me finish." This technique will make everyone feel uncomfortable—especially you—but it is worth it. You will feel terrific when you stand up for your ideas. After you have done this at two or three meetings, your colleague will begin to recognize your strength, and so will the managers.

Points to remember when dealing with Credit-Stealers:

Be assertive.

Document your work.

Be professional.

Face the Credit-Stealer.

Use "I" language.

Become more visible.

Blow your own horn.

Give credit where credit is due.

Don't believe that the credit-stealing will change by itself.

Stay in the Freedom State.

• KNOW-ALLS—HOW TO AVOID FEELING OR LOOKING IGNORANT WHEN DEALING WITH A KNOW-ALL

Know-Alls are people who always have the perfect answer, at least in their own minds. They are insensitive to anyone's opinion except their own. Most of the time they are aggressive and loud. There are two varieties of Know-All:

1. The first type of Know-All actually does know most or all the answers. She is smart and has a way of pushing her projects or ideas through to completion. Her style of communication is rude, obnoxious, and condescending. She has no use for your input.

2. The second type of Know-All is "all headlines and no news." He will act as if he has the answers to everything, but most of the time his facts are incorrect or unresearched. You may learn the hard way that he is a phony, because he sounds so convincing. He will not take any responsibility for his mistakes and will have a mile-long list of plausible reasons as to why the mistake was not his fault.

Here are some basic strategies for dealing with the first type of Know-All:

1. Be prepared.

2. Listen carefully.

3. Don't make mistakes.

4. Double-check all your work and facts. This type of Know-All is influenced by facts.

5. Give her all the power she wants. Let her know that you feel she has all the right answers and that you are willing to let her run the show.

6. Ask specific questions based on your knowledge and research of the issue.

7. Don't challenge, but offer alternative ideas if you know he is wrong.

8. Let her save face if she is wrong.

9. Make friends, not enemies.

Spending time with this Know-All can be boring, because your only entertainment will be her stories of her all-embracing knowledge. If you bring up a subject that she is unfamiliar with she will change the topic quickly back to her sizable area of expertise. You need to decide how important this relationship is to you. If it is not valuable for your career or personal life, it could be a waste of time and energy.

Try these basic strategies for dealing with the second type of Know-All:

1. Ask questions. Get him to elaborate. Remember that he is all headlines and no news and therefore he will soon run out of back-up information.

2. Blow his cover if you are an expert, but be aware that he may go on the attack.

3. Cope with him alone.

4. Point out that his opinions may not be accurate, while leaving his giant-size ego intact.

5. Correct him in a meeting only when you have no other choice. Be gentle and move on to another topic.

6. Decide if it is worth your time to be with this person.

SITUATION 4. The problem I have relates to another manager of equal status. He believes he is the expert on all work-related matters, due to his age and length of time in the firm. He is smart but very obnoxious. He does not listen to the viewpoints of other staff members at all. *Evan.*

This person is a type 1 Know-All. Evan must start by realizing that he can't change him. What he needs to know is how he can improve the work relationship and feel better when communicating with this manager. Here are some steps I would advise him to follow:

1. Don't play at one-upmanship with this person: you will not win.

2. Make him believe that you look up to him. Support his ego. Why? Because when he sees you on his side, he will begin to bring you in as an equal. He will trust you.

3. When you or another member of staff wishes to have a viewpoint heard, suggest your idea and ask his opinion on it.

4. Do not be confrontational.

5. This may sound very difficult, but it will work. Making friends with the enemy will make teamwork easier. It will take some time for this manager to trust the change. When he does, he will stop acting so aggressively.

SITUATION 5. My father-in-law demands and expects respect but gives none. He is a big Know-All, Know Nothing. There is only one way to think—his way. He is loud, and is positive he is always correct. *Naomi.*

This man is a type 2 Know-All. Because he is a relative, my solution is to leave him alone. If Naomi deflates his ego, she will ruin the possibility of any type of relationship. If what he is preaching affects her specifically, then she might respond by seeking further explanation—for example: "I am interested in why you think that is the only way to do this." Or: "Give me more information about your idea—it sounds interesting." When she asks him to explain, she should do so with an air of interest and some confusion. She should not attack. As a last resort, she should spend as little time with him as possible.

SITUATION 6. A client complains about not receiving a message on his pager. I establish that he was working in an area where transmission cannot be guaranteed. The client will not listen to any explanation. He is very single-minded and always feels he is right. His superior attitude makes it hard to work with him. *Larry.*

This Know-All has made a mistake and does not want to hear about it. Proving him wrong only helps to prove that he can be obnoxious. Here are some steps that Larry might take:

1. Apologize for his inconvenience: "I am sure it is very frustrating to miss a call."

2. Continue by discussing the problem with interest, not putting him in the wrong. For example: "Do you spend a lot of time in this area?"

3. Ask questions, such as: "How do you usually cope in this area when you need your messages? . . . Okay, that sounds like a good idea."

4. Offer helpful solutions: "One of my other clients who has the same problem handles it by . . . Does this sound like something you could do?"

There is no guarantee that this Know-All client will ever become easy to work with. As Larry deals with him with more confidence, he will feel better and will be less likely to become a victim.

Points to remember when dealing with type 1 Know-Alls:

Don't attempt one-upmanship.

Acknowledge intellect.

Ask for the Know-All's opinion of a new idea.

Do not confront.

Do not make mistakes.

Give him or her power.

Ask questions.

Let the person save face.

Stay calm.

Points to remember when dealing with type 2 Know-Alls:

Ask probing questions, gently.

Sound interested.

Don't confront.

Talk to the Know-All.

Be gentle with his or her ego.

Leave the person alone.

• SHOW-OFFS—HOW TO KEEP THEIR FLAMBOYANT BEHAVIOR FROM FOOLING YOU WHILE GETTING MORE CONTROL OF THE SITUATION

Show-Offs are usually the life and soul of the party. They will do almost anything to get attention, whether at a social event or a business meeting. They talk more than they should and stay longer than you want them to. They can exude an aura of success but it may not go deeper than the flamboyant exterior behavior. Don't let them fool you. They have such a desire to impress that they may do almost anything, even if it is embarrassing. The Show-Off seems conceited and will blow his horn about his achievements. However, as in many of the other difficult behaviors, he usually shows off because he does not feel good about himself.

Lee is a Show-Off. She can be picked out of any crowd by her loud laugh. She has used her show-off ability to get many jobs but is always found out by her poor performance. A first impression of Lee is outgoing, fun, energetic, knowledgeable, and interesting. How could such a good impression be so wrong? Because Lee has perfected showing off, but has not developed the follow-through to prove the first impression correct.

Lee began a new job with her usual show-off enthusiasm. Her colleague, Lynn, was happy to have a new woman to work with. Lynn began helping with anything she could in order to make Lee part of the team. In a short time, Lynn discovered that Lee did not know much about anything and was attempting to get just enough information from Lynn to keep her show-off performance believable. Lynn decided that this had to stop. Lee became angry and vindictive, and did her best to discredit Lynn. Lynn, unsure at first of what to do, decided to document her own ideas so that Lee did not take the credit, then to stay quiet and let Lee bury herself. It took two years, but finally everyone saw through Lee's show-off act and she was asked to leave.

Show-Offs can be delightful and have little effect on others. However, as shown in the story above, Show-Offs can also be destructive if not discovered and dealt with appropriately. Lynn's mistake in dealing with Lee was to immediately believe everything she saw. Sitting back for a while and observing Lee's behavior might have helped Lynn avoid this trap.

Try these basic strategies for dealing with Show-Offs:

1. Don't be fooled by the Show-Off's self-confident appearance.

2. Tease him in a gentle way about his flamboyant behavior.

3. Don't be tempted to outdo a Show-off.

4. Find out where the Show-Off is actually successful, and compliment her. You'll win her true friendship by building her up in a sincere way. This will encourage her to show off her real successes.

5. Listen carefully so that you can ask the right questions to get at the truth.

6. Plan specific times for meetings to start and finish. Stick to these times.

7. Give the Show-Off the platform he desires. Get him to lead a meeting with a very tight agenda.

8. Take notes during conversations to show that you are documenting the information.

9. Tape-record conversations. This will stop the
   Show-Off saying things he or she does not want to
   be responsible for later.

SITUATION 7. My employee is a nice guy. Good to be with at parties but somewhat disastrous at work. He needs to show off and be everyone's friend. He causes chaos administratively. *Joseph.*

This Show-Off is difficult to deal with because he is so nice and fun to be with. It sounds as if he thinks he is still at college. He is an example of the Immature State described in Chapter 3. So how can Joseph improve the work situation without destroying the person?

1. Take an authoritative position.

2. Stop being his friend and start being the boss.

3. Talk with him one to one.

4. Set standards and expectations.

5. Get him to keep track of his progress through a
   time log or a written weekly report.

6. Stay in the Freedom State when managing him. Do
   not go into the Controlling State regardless of his
   response.

7. Be careful not to regress to being too friendly when
   his performance improves.

8. Use the model in Chapter 4.

SITUATION 8. This employee is full of confidence—actually too much confidence. He is always blowing his own horn. I am having difficulty getting him to realize that he does not know as much as he thinks. I don't want to damage his ego. *Julie.*

Getting this employee to understand that he is not as smart as he thinks he is will be impossible without destroying him. This is a typical problem when dealing with a Show-Off. It is not important for Julie to get him to accept what she knows to be true—that he is a Show-Off. It *is* important to have the job done well and to give credit where credit is due. How can Julie do that?

1. Stop caring that he blows his own horn. Realize that anyone with eyes and ears knows that he is a Show-Off.

2. Ask questions about his knowledge in order to clarify things: "Where did you get the information?" "What do you have to substantiate that fact?" "Why are you sure this will work?" "How do you plan to proceed?" "Who will work with you on this project?"

3. Stay in the Freedom State. He may become angry when his knowledge is questioned. Do not let it keep you from questioning, but do stay calm and nonconfrontational.

4. Stay silent when he is full of self-admiration. When he has finished blowing his horn, continue with whatever you need to say as if he had not spoken.

SITUATION 9. An employee who does everything he can to make me and others look stupid. When he is given a task, he contemplates whether he wants to do it or not, and whether it is up to his standard. He delights in telling everyone else how, what, and when things should be done. *Keith.*

This Show-Off is not one of the "nice ones." His attitude is superior and his method is control. He seems to need to build himself up by making others look stupid. There is an old adage that is appropriate here: "No one can make you look stupid without your permission." It is not easy to stop this type of Show-Off but with consistency it can be done.

There were three specific problems mentioned in Situation 9:

1. *Tries to make others look stupid.* Keith should stop him immediately, every time. He must ask why he does it and tell him that no one appreciates being put down. Following this confrontation, he will probably do it again. Keith should be prepared to come back as many times as necessary. He should say to himself, "Never again will I be made to look stupid!" and then follow through.

2. *Contemplates whether a task is up to his standard before doing it.* There is a definite attitude problem here. Unless he is the boss or the authority, there should be no alternative for this employee but to do his job. The request should be stated clearly in an assertive manner: "This is what I need on Project A. When will you be able to complete the work—by Friday noon or Monday 9 A.M.?" If the employee ignores the request or does not want to do it, Keith should go back to the original question: "You may have misunderstood me. There is not a choice about doing the work, just a choice about when you plan to finish. Which day will you have it completed?" Keith should continue to repeat his request until he gets a satisfactory response. When this employee realizes that his show-off attitude will not be tolerated, he will change or leave.

3. *Tells everyone how to do the job.* If his information is genuinely helpful, Keith should thank him and get on with the work. If his way is no more correct

than Keith's, a good response might be: "Thank you, I can see you really want to help; however, I am going to do it the way I had decided." Keith should kill him with kindness, and have something waiting for him to do—another project, research—whenever he wants to interfere in someone else's work.

This whole situation is another example of how the Show-Off needs attention to feel good about himself, and of how he claims it at the expense of others.

Points to remember when dealing with a Show-Off:

Don't be fooled by appearance.

Don't try for one-upmanship.

Support the Show-Off's "real" successes.

Take notes to keep this person honest.

Respond to desired behavior—don't react to the show-off behavior.

Stay in the Freedom State.

CHAPTER TEN

MALE-FEMALE COMMUNICATION DIFFERENCES

We have talked about many different types of difficult behavior in a variety of jobs and situations. The examples used demonstrate communication man to man, woman to woman, and man to woman. However, the innate differences between men and women can make for challenging situations regardless of any other circumstances. The male body and mind are significantly different from the female body and mind. Men have developed and counted on their physical strength for centuries, while women have grown to rely on their emotional strength. Knowing this intellectually and also seeing the differences physically does not stop us from ignoring these differences when we communicate. We think that the opposite sex has the same reality as we do. We believe that they think the same and come to similar conclusions. We look for the same signals from the opposite sex as we ourselves give. If the response from the opposite sex to our communication is different from that which we anticipated, we can become confused, angry, withdrawn, or even hostile. In fact, if we could learn to listen to the opposite sex with the interest and understanding that we have when we listen to someone from another culture or speaking another language we would improve our communication dramatically.

The following are examples of the different attitudes of men and women in the workplace, and possible solutions for improving communication and understanding between the sexes.

Men focus on one thing at a time.
Women focus on many things at one time.

Men: Understand that women's talents are different from yours. Acknowledge their ability to do many things well and stop considering them scattered or unfocused.

Women: Understand that men do one thing at a time because it gives them the best results. Do not consider them slow but look at them instead as guaranteeing perfect results. This means they can be relied on.

Men live by "If its not broken, don't fix it."
Women feel limited if things stay the same, because their world is mobile.

Men: View the ever-changing world of women as an opportunity to improve and to grow to new levels. Understand that to keep things the same makes women feel stagnated. Stop viewing a woman's need for freedom as just a way to avoid boredom.

Women: Understand that men feel they are in control by leaving things the way they are. They feel satisfied, allowing them to work on areas that they view as broken. Do not think of men in this situation as afraid or insecure about change.

Men prefer structure.
Women feel manipulated and dominated by the imposition of structure.

Men: Understand that supporting women by not imposing structure will improve their productivity dramatically.

Women: Understand that structure is important to a man for his own self-respect and for respect from other men. Women can work better with men by presenting their ideas in a structured way.

Men need a step-by-step process.
Women jump over steps if they feel they are not needed, or take the steps out of the traditional male order.

Men: Relax and realize that this untraditional process works for women and will result in an appropriate conclusion. Trust more.

Women: Be patient when the male process takes longer than the female process. Realize that it works overall. Trust more.

Men will make a decision and it is final.
Women will make provisional decisions. After a while, they may decide to change their minds if the decision does not feel appropriate.

Men: This one can drive you crazy, but don't let it. Ask questions: "Are you discussing this plan as a means to making your final decision?" Often a woman will not be sure if she is making a decision or not until after she has stated her case. Treat women, in this situation, as if they were speaking another language.

Women: Realize that a decision made by a male is final. This is not preparatory talk for a later decision. If you are not happy, state your need for more discussion before a decision is agreed on.

Men when they initiate change will plan the amount of energy needed to accomplish the change.
Women jump into change and gain energy from the process.

Men: Understand that just when you think the woman is drained of energy, this is when she will initiate a new change, perhaps rearranging the office for a better work environment, or beginning a new project. The words "tired" or "low energy" do not mean finished for a woman. Be excited by their spurt of energy.

Women: Understand that men must plan how much energy they will expend on a given project. Let them know in advance what you need and expect. Do not add a major "to do" list just when the man thinks he is done. Be considerate.

Men tend to go inside themselves to restore energy.
Women tend to go outside themselves to restore energy.

Men: Understand that when a woman is tired she will tend to talk to friends, tell stories, or ask for feedback. Through this process women gain energy and can probably start again.

Women: Understand that men need to be quiet and possibly alone to regain energy. Do not chat with them when you see they are tired. You will not have their attention and they may even think you are a nuisance.

Men segregate issues into parts to arrive at their solutions.
Women approach issues with an overview to arrive at their solutions.

Men: Understand that women need the whole picture before making a decision. If you tell them that they don't need to know everything, you will be alienating them from your team and also making it very difficult for them to come up with solutions.

Women: Understand that giving men the whole picture can be frustrating. They need to work on one segment at a time. If you work from the overview perspective, they may see you as a dreamer or too pushy.

Men view "wants" and "can haves" as the same.
Women see "wants" and "can haves" as separate conditions.

Men: Understanding this difference could change your life. When a woman talks about "wants" she does not necessarily need or expect to have them. She can be fantasizing or dreaming, without any expectations, and wants you to do this with her. It does not mean that you are responsible for fulfilling these "wants."

Women: Understanding this item could change your life too. If a man talks about "wants" this is not a fantasy. He will take steps to bring them into reality or "can haves." Realize that these wants are serious and will probably happen. Also be aware that when you talk about "wants," men may seem unresponsive if they are afraid that they will be made responsible for fulfilling your desires.

Men focus on techniques that will produce results.
Women focus on the process first, with the results as a by-product.

Men: Understand that women are always processing. This is why they can jump ahead and do steps out of order. They will achieve the results needed but are more focused on the process. When communicating, be less bottom-line with women and you will get better results. Relax.

Women: Understand that men are focused on results. Communicate from the results backward: this will enable you to discuss the techniques needed to achieve the results.

The difference between men and women in this particular area can help to explain why women become so stressed over the preparations for a holiday, while men are fairly relaxed. While women are preoccupied about getting everything ready, men see only the arrival at the destination and all the consequent enjoyment.

Men talk about issues in order to resolve them.
Women talk about issues in order to express themselves.

Men: Understand that women will communicate just to "trouble-talk." This does not mean that anything must be solved; it means they just need to be heard. If you are confused, ask them whether what they are saying is trouble-talking, or whether they actually need to resolve the situation. You may be surprised.

Women: Understanding this innate difference will help you to accept why a man does not tell you everything. If he can't resolve a situation, he will probably not share it with you. If you keep pushing him to tell you what is on his mind, it will probably make him angry, because he sees no solution. Talking to you about it only makes him feel more responsible for resolving it.

Men evaluate good teamwork by how little the team members need to talk to each other.
Women evaluate good teamwork by the ability to have ongoing communication with all members.

Men: If you are in a team with women, be willing to discuss processes more. Discuss where you are, where you want to end up, and how you will get there. Women believe that teamwork means there will be more communication than usual. If you fail to discuss the process, they will feel you are shutting them out.

Women: Understand that just because you are working on a team with men, it does not mean they will share everything with you. Do not take their silence personally. Ask specific questions and expect shorter answers than you want.

Men smile less, causing them to be seen as strong and powerful but not warm and supportive.
Women smile more, inviting interruption and causing them to be seen less as leaders but more approachable and helpful.

Men: Understand that women are naturally warmer and more supportive in the work environment. This does not mean that they are poor leaders or cannot take the full responsibility of a management position. Enjoy their smiles along with their ability to do many things at a time. Smile more yourselves, and women will react by supporting your decisions.

Women: Understand that the stern face of a male is a symbol of power. Do not expect that your wonderful personality will soften him, and, in fact, when in the presence of an unsmiling leader, smile less yourself.

The styles of communication that men and women use make sense given the way we learned them. However, they each have different consequences in the workplace, as Deborah Tannen writes in her book *Talking from 9 to 5*. In order to avoid being put in the one-down position, many men have developed strategies for making sure they get the one-up position. This way of communicating serves them well when it comes to hiring and promotion. Women are more likely to speak in styles that are less effective in getting recognized and promoted. If they speak in the styles that men use, being assertive, sounding sure of themselves, talking up what they have done to make sure they get credit for it, they run the risk of not being liked or being seen as too aggressive or bitchy. Men who are not very aggressive and communicate in the way women are expected to communicate can be thought of as "wimps" or as lacking self-confidence.

Ritual apologies illustrate another difference in communication styles of men and women. Deborah Tannen writes that admitting fault can be experienced as taking a one-down position. When both parties share the blame, they end up on an equal footing. That is the logic behind the ritual sharing of blame in response to an apology. It's a mutual face-saving device. However, when someone does not use apologies in this way, he may take the apology literally, and this can lead to resentment on the part of the apologizer. Tannen states that if I say, "I'm sorry," and you say, "I accept your apology," then my attempt to achieve balance has misfired, and I think you have put me in a one-down position, though you probably think I put myself there. Research has shown that women are much more likely to apologize than men, and that women's apologies are especially likely to result in putting them down.

I have observed many examples of the differences in ritual

apologies. Here is an example from a training session just completed. In the session there were five women and one man. Tom was elected to be the recorder, to write what was being discussed on a flip chart. As he approached the chart, the others stated what great writing he had and how good he would be at this job. He just proceeded without comment. Tom never apologized, even when he made a mistake or had to ask for help; he just did his job. Following Tom, two women had the opportunity to write. Mary began apologizing as she walked to the chart. "I'm sorry, my spelling may be wrong, and my writing is terrible." Beverly also apologized. "I'm sorry, I am so tall this may look awkward. I don't know if you will be able to read what I write."

The negative effect of apologizing frequently when there is no real reason is that it puts the person in a one-down position, lowering them in the opinion of others and also hurting their self-esteem. When I pointed this behavior out to the group, the women recognized it and said, "Yeah, why do we always do that?" They also said, "Tom didn't apologize." It is a habit, taught to us by gender and culture. The first step in changing it is awareness.

Remember, working with a member of the opposite sex can be as difficult as working with someone from another culture. Do not expect that just because you think one way, everyone else should agree. Your reality may work for you, but each person has their own reality, based on their gender, heritage, and experiences.

All of the differences described in this chapter are the average. There will certainly be variations and sometimes you may find the tables turned completely, the male taking on female characteristics and vice versa.

Be patient, understanding, and be willing to look at their perception and watch the wonderful changes in all the people around you.

ACTION WORKBOOK

You now have all the information you need to make a difference in your most difficult situation. What will you do with it? Will you hope that by reading the information you will automatically know what to do? Or will you buy another copy of this book, highlight your most difficult person and give the book to them anonymously, hoping they will change?

There is only one thing you can do to change your situation permanently. Take action! Plan the exact steps you need in order to improve each relationship. This has been made easy for you. The following Action Outline gives you the appropriate questions to answer regarding each difficult situation you are dealing with. By filling in the answers, you will begin the process of solving the problem.

Who are my most difficult persons?

1. _____

2. _____

3. _____

What do they do that causes me to find them difficult? Describe the behavior. Be specific._____

_____

_____

_____

Which type of difficult behavior from this book do they most closely typify? Check the relevant category.

HOSTILE-AGGRESSIVE _____

Explosives _____

Insulting Attackers_____

Hidden Sarcasm_____

PASSIVE-AGGRESSIVE _____

Silent Judges_____

Avoiders _____

Information-Keepers _____

PROCRASTINATING _____

Untruthfuls _____

Idlers _____

Perfectionists _____

NEGATIVE-COMPLAINING _____

Whiners _____

Idea-Destroyers _____

Guilt-Givers _____

ARROGANT _____
Credit-Stealers _____
Know-Alls _____
Show-Offs _____

MALE-FEMALE DIFFERENCES_____
_____
_____
_____

Which strategies will I use to improve my situation? Review the chapter describing the category you checked._____
_____
_____
_____

How do my difficult persons view me? Am I their difficult person? Be honest._____
_____
_____
_____

What types of communicators are they? Check appropriate category.

Bumper Sticker Communicator? _____
Caretaking Communicator? _____
Cellular Phone Communicator? _____
Technocratic Communicator? _____

What type of communicator am I?

Bumper Sticker Communicator? _____
Caretaking Communicator? _____
Cellular Phone Communicator? _____
Technocratic Communicator? _____

Do our styles conflict? If so, how?_____

_____

_____

_____

How can I communicate to help my difficult persons hear me? Should
I talk more . . . talk less . . . more technical . . . more caring?_____

_____

_____

_____

How do I react to my difficult persons' behavior?_____

_____

_____

_____

How do they hook me?_____

_____

_____

_____

Which state do I use to respond? Check one.

Freedom State _____
Immature State _____
Controlling State _____

What can I do to stay in the Freedom State?_____

_____

_____

_____

What do I want to say to my difficult persons?_____

_____

_____

_____

Now act out what you want to say. Play both parts: Be yourself as you
will speak to each of your difficult persons. Now respond as you pre-
dict your difficult persons will._____

_____

_____

_____

What problems should I be prepared for?

1. _____
2. _____
3. _____
4. _____

Now, how can I prevent or solve these problems?

1. _____
2. _____
3. _____
4. _____

CONCLUSION

In conclusion, I want to discuss the most important thread that is woven throughout this book. It is not the fact that there are many different types of problem people. It is not a collection of ways and techniques available to change them into wonderful, delightful work associates or friends. The most important thing that I hope you have discovered from reading this book and working on the Action Workbook is that you cannot expect your problem person to change by wishing he or she would do so. There is no magic wand in this book. The only person who can actually change things is you. All the strategies in this book are designed to help you approach or avoid problem people. You can stop being a victim, reduce your anger, stress, and frustration, and feel better about the communication with all the problem people in your life.

Here is one last story demonstrating that we are the only ones who can change.

I sent the senior vice president, whom I mentioned in the introduction to this book, a copy of the manuscript. Shortly afterward, I received a call that demonstrated that he had not changed over the years, as I had always hoped he would. There was the familiar attacking behavior that had always pushed my button and made me feel inadequate. But this call also showed that I had changed. I was able to take a deep breath and respond in a way that did not hook me or cause me increased stress. This is how the call went:

Ted: Ted Cooper. Have a minute? *(Not friendly, abrupt.)*

Marilyn: Sure, Ted. It's been at least a year since we last spoke. How are you?

Ted (no acknowledgment of this statement or time past): Marilyn, first of all, you should know how to spell my name by now. It really makes me angry that you mispelled my name on the envelope.

Marilyn: Oops, you'd think I would have got it right after all these years. It must be a subconscious problem. *(Before, this would have put me under, feeling totally ridiculous. This time I felt a little embarrassed but it felt funny not horrible and devastating.)*

Ted: Let me tell you the other mistakes I found. There is a misspelled word on page one, and another somewhere on page three.

Marilyn: Gee, Ted, I didn't know you were an editor too!

Ted: Well, I didn't want you to be embarrassed when you sent it to your publisher.

Marilyn: I have not sent it yet, Ted. My concern is content.

Ted: I don't remember the situation referred to in your introduction, but I'm sure you've recalled it accurately, since it affected you.

Marilyn: Yes, Ted, telling me I would not make the grade on my first day on a new job does tend to be remembered. I am glad you can acknowledge that. That statement, Ted, was a whole new beginning for me. I learned to look at the workplace with a different perspective. If you had not said that, this book might never have been born. *(You never know when something that was intended to be hurtful can actually inspire growth.)*

Marilyn: Thanks, Ted. *(A little small talk and the conversation ended.)*

Ted was still the same person, but I was not hooked! I avoided reacting and feeling as if I were his victim. When I hung the phone up, I thought, *Wow! People don't change, no matter how long you wait, no matter how much you want them to, unless you communicate the information in a way that forces them to respond differently.*

Whatever situation you are dealing with, discover your solution in this book, and develop your understanding of the strategies by completing the Action Workbook, by attending classes or seminars, by listening to tapes, or by any other means that works for you. Once you have found your solution, work on it every day. When you get hooked by a problem person, just stop, take a breath, and think how you want it to be next time. Then be prepared, because there will always be a next time.

BIBLIOGRAPHY

Blanchard, Kenneth, and Spencer Johnson. *The One Minute Manager*. New York: Berkley Books, 1982.

Cava, Roberta. *Dealing with Difficult People*. London: Piatkus Books, 1990. Toronto, Ontario: Key Porter Books, 1990.

Cohen, Herb. *You Can Negotiate Anything*. New York: Bantam Books, 1987.

Fournies, Ferdinand F. *Coaching for Improved Work Performance*. New York: Liberty Hall Press, an imprint of McGraw-Hill Inc., 1987.

Littauer, Florence. *How to Understand Others by Understanding Yourself, Personality Plus*. Old Tappan, N.J.: Fleming H. Revell Company, 1983.

Pfeiffer, J. W., and J. E. Jones, eds. *A Handbook of Structured Experiences for Human Relations Training,* Vol. IV. San Diego, Ca.: Pfeiffer and Company, 1973.

Solomon, Muriel. *Working With Difficult People*. Englewood Cliffs, N.J.: Prentice-Hall, 1990.

Tanenbaum, Joe. *Male and Female Realities*. Sugarland, Tex.: Candle Publishing Company, 1989.

Tannen, Deborah. *You Just Don't Understand Me*. Geneva, Ill.: Ball Publishing, 1991.

Tannen, Deborah. *Talking 9 to 5*. New York: William Morrow, 1994.

INDEX

ABOUT THE AUTHOR

Marilyn Wheeler is the founder and president of Marilyn Wheeler and Associates, a personal and professional development company devoted to management training, corporate seminars, and motivational speaking. A much-sought-after speaker, Wheeler has traveled from the United States to Australia, France, Greece, New Zealand, South Africa, and the United Kingdom to address professionals on a variety of topics.

In the United States, Wheeler has worked for such Fortune 500 companies as Pacific Bell, Mattel Toys, Royal Cruise Line, Hughes Aircraft, JCPenney, and Sheraton, among others. Her seminars are aimed at business professionals interested in developing and improving managerial skills through such workshops as How to Deal with Problem People at Work, Giving Feedback to

Improve Performance, Managing Employees Through Change, Developing High Performance Work Teams, and Risk Taking–Surviving Change. Since 1987, thousands of people have enjoyed and been motivated to achieve their potential by Marilyn's warmth, honesty, and straightforward style of communicating.

Marilyn Wheeler's career spans twenty-five years as a business professional, working with a host of national and international companies. As Director of Marketing for the California Mart, home to more than 2,100 manufacturers and commercial wholesalers, Wheeler supervised and trained a staff of thirty involved in the successful execution of all trade shows. She has also worked with the International Trade Commissions from France, Italy, Hong Kong, Sweden, and Great Britain. Prior to founding her own firm, Wheeler served as Vice President of Diane Freis, a well-known couturier and manufacturer headquartered in Hong Kong.

The first edition of Wheeler's book *Problem People at Work and How to Deal with Them* has been published already in Australia, New Zealand, South Africa, and the United Kingdom.

You can contact Marilyn Wheeler for seminars, training, or consulting by writing to:

Marilyn Wheeler & Associates
5318 E. Second St., Suite 320
Long Beach, CA 90803

or by fax/phone at (310) 987-1237